TEENAGE SEXUALITY

OPPOSING VIEWPOINTS ®

Ken R. Wells, *Book Editor*

Bonnie Szumski, *Publisher*
Helen Cothran, *Managing Editor*

OPPOSING
VIEWPOINTS®
SERIES

GREENHAVEN PRESS
An imprint of Thomson Gale, a part of The Thomson Corporation

THOMSON

━━━━━━✳━━━━━━™

GALE

Detroit • New York • San Francisco • San Diego • New Haven, Conn.
Waterville, Maine • London • Munich

THOMSON

——————— ✦ ———————™

GALE

LIBRARY OF CONGRESS CATALOGING-IN-PUBLICATION DATA

Teenage sexuality / Ken R. Wells, book editor.
    p. cm. — (Opposing viewpoints)
  Includes bibliographical references and index.
  ISBN 0-7377-3362-4 (lib. bdg. : alk. paper) —
  ISBN 0-7377-3363-2 (pbk. : alk. paper)
    1. Teenagers—United States—Sexual behavior. 2. Teenagers—United
  States—Attitudes. 3. Sex instruction—United States. I. Wells, Ken R. II. Opposing
  viewpoints series (Unnumbered)
  HQ27.T422 2006
  306.70835—dc22   2005052664

> "Congress shall make no law. . . abridging the freedom of speech, or of the press."

First Amendment to the U.S. Constitution

The basic foundation of our democracy is the First Amendment guarantee of freedom of expression. The Opposing Viewpoints Series is dedicated to the concept of this basic freedom and the idea that it is more important to practice it than to enshrine it.

Contents

Why Consider Opposing Viewpoints?

"The only way in which a human being can make some approach to knowing the whole of a subject is by hearing what can be said about it by persons of every variety of opinion and studying all modes in which it can be looked at by every character of mind. No wise man ever acquired his wisdom in any mode but this."

John Stuart Mill

In our media-intensive culture it is not difficult to find differing opinions. Thousands of newspapers and magazines and dozens of radio and television talk shows resound with differing points of view. The difficulty lies in deciding which opinion to agree with and which "experts" seem the most credible. The more inundated we become with differing opinions and claims, the more essential it is to hone critical reading and thinking skills to evaluate these ideas. Opposing Viewpoints books address this problem directly by presenting stimulating debates that can be used to enhance and teach these skills. The varied opinions contained in each book examine many different aspects of a single issue. While examining these conveniently edited opposing views, readers can develop critical thinking skills such as the ability to compare and contrast authors' credibility, facts, argumentation styles, use of persuasive techniques, and other stylistic tools. In short, the Opposing Viewpoints Series is an ideal way to attain the higher-level thinking and reading skills so essential in a culture of diverse and contradictory opinions.

In addition to providing a tool for critical thinking, Opposing Viewpoints books challenge readers to question their own strongly held opinions and assumptions. Most people form their opinions on the basis of upbringing, peer pressure, and personal, cultural, or professional bias. By reading carefully balanced opposing views, readers must directly confront new ideas as well as the opinions of those with whom they disagree. This is not to simplistically argue that everyone who reads opposing views will—or should—change his or her opinion. Instead, the series enhances readers' understanding of their own views by encouraging confrontation with opposing ideas. Careful examination of others' views can lead to the readers' understanding of the logical inconsistencies in their own opinions, perspective on why they hold an opinion, and the consideration of the possibility that their opinion requires further evaluation.

Evaluating Other Opinions

To ensure that this type of examination occurs, Opposing Viewpoints books present all types of opinions. Prominent spokespeople on different sides of each issue as well as well-known professionals from many disciplines challenge the reader. An additional goal of the series is to provide a forum for other, less known, or even unpopular viewpoints. The opinion of an ordinary person who has had to make the decision to cut off life support from a terminally ill relative, for example, may be just as valuable and provide just as much insight as a medical ethicist's professional opinion. The editors have two additional purposes in including these less known views. One, the editors encourage readers to respect others' opinions—even when not enhanced by professional credibility. It is only by reading or listening to and objectively evaluating others' ideas that one can determine whether they are worthy of consideration. Two, the inclusion of such viewpoints encourages the important critical thinking skill of objectively evaluating an author's credentials and bias. This evaluation will illuminate an author's reasons for taking a particular stance on an issue and will aid in readers' evaluation of the author's ideas.

It is our hope that these books will give readers a deeper understanding of the issues debated and an appreciation of the complexity of even seemingly simple issues when good and honest people disagree. This awareness is particularly important in a democratic society such as ours in which people enter into public debate to determine the common good. Those with whom one disagrees should not be regarded as enemies but rather as people whose views deserve careful examination and may shed light on one's own.

Thomas Jefferson once said that "difference of opinion leads to inquiry, and inquiry to truth." Jefferson, a broadly educated man, argued that "if a nation expects to be ignorant and free . . . it expects what never was and never will be." As individuals and as a nation, it is imperative that we consider the opinions of others and examine them with skill and discernment. The Opposing Viewpoints Series is intended to help readers achieve this goal.

David L. Bender and Bruno Leone,
Founders

Introduction

"Sex education in [western European] countries begins with the assumption that young people will carry on a number of sexual relationships during their teen years and initiate sex play short of intercourse long before that, which they do, and that sexual expression is a healthy and happy part of growing up."

—*Author Judith Levine*, Harmful to Minors:
The Perils of Protecting Children from Sex

Judith Levine, author of *Harmful to Minors: The Perils of Protecting Children from Sex*, has documented a great chasm between western European and American attitudes toward teen sexuality. Whereas western Europeans generally view teen sex as natural and healthy, many Americans view it as dangerous, even immoral. Research into issues related to teen sex document great differences between western European and American youths, which many experts attribute to this disparity in attitudes toward teen sexual activity.

Statistics show that in two key categories, American teens are more comparable to their counterparts in eastern Europe than in western Europe. Countries with the highest teenage birthrates among the world's developed nations are Armenia, Bulgaria, Georgia, Moldova, Ukraine, and the United States. Countries with the lowest teenage birthrates are Belgium, Denmark, Finland, Italy, Japan, the Netherlands, Slovenia, Spain, and Sweden. Countries with the highest teenage abortion rates are Bulgaria, Estonia, Hungary, Latvia, Romania, Russia, and the United States. Countries with the lowest teenage abortion rates are Belgium, Germany, Ireland, Israel, Italy, Japan, the Netherlands, and Spain.

In America the teen pregnancy rate per 1,000 women ages 15–19 is nearly 80, significantly higher than in France (20.2), Germany (16.1), and the Netherlands (8.7). The birthrate per 1,000 women ages 15–19 is 48.7 in the United States, 12.5 in Germany, 10 in France, and 4.5 in the Netherlands. The abortion rate for the same group is 27.5 in the United

States, 10.2 in France, 4.2 in the Netherlands, and 3.6 in Germany.

When it comes to sexually transmitted diseases (STDs), the figures for U.S. teens are high when compared to western Europe. The percentage of men ages 15–24 infected with HIV is 0.75 in the United States compared to only 0.49 in France, 0.27 in the Netherlands, and 0.14 in Germany. The gonorrhea rate per 100,000 teens ages 15–19 is 571.8 in the United States, about 12 in Germany, and 7.7 in France and the Netherlands.

Why is there such a vast difference in teen sex statistics between America and western Europe? Many researchers say the answers are complex. "It may be the case that they (western Europeans) have better sex and HIV education programs," claims Douglas Kirby, a researcher formerly with the National Campaign to Prevent Teen Pregnancy.

> It's certainly the case that in most of the western European countries they have a more homogeneous population, which has reached greater agreement on what values should be emphasized to young people. Those tend, typically, to be pretty liberal values. But there's much greater agreement upon them than there is in the United States, where we have real polarization. So in Western European countries, (teens are) consistently given a common message, whereas in the U.S. we give conflicting messages.

Mike Males, a sociologist at the University of California at Santa Cruz, agrees. According to Males, teens hear contradictory messages from adults, who "bellow morality but indulge (in) promiscuity."

Melissa Harris, a senior at Northwestern University, was eighteen when she went on a two-week tour of Europe as part of a group of Americans to examine the European approach to teen sexuality. She said that compared to Europe, American teens live in a society where sex and being sexual is filled with shame, guilt, and fear tactics. "Sex in the Netherlands, Germany, and France is a public health issue, not a moral one," she says. "It's about protecting your partner and protecting yourself."

The nonprofit group Advocates for Youth has identified what it considers the European attitudes toward teens and teenage sexuality that help protect adolescent sexual health.

According to the organization, adults in the Netherlands, France, and Germany view young people as assets, not problems. Adults value and respect adolescents and expect teens to act responsibly. Advocates for Youth also claims that in western Europe, research is the basis for public policies to reduce unintended pregnancies, abortions, and STDs. Political and religious groups have little influence on public health policy. Moreover, families have open, honest, and consistent discussions with teens about sex and support the role of educators and health care providers in making sexual health information and services available for teens. "European countries are very comfortable with the idea of teen sexuality. It's not considered taboo, as is the case here in the U.S.," said Barbara Hubeman, director of outreach and education at Advocates for Youth. "Society doesn't view adolescent sexual behavior from a moral perspective in these countries. They don't debate whether teen sex should or should not occur, but they discuss the ways to keep teens as educated and safe as possible."

Authors of the viewpoints in *Opposing Viewpoints: Teenage Sexuality* explore issues such as teen pregnancy, sexually transmitted diseases, and sex education in the following chapters: What Factors Influence Teen Attitudes Toward Sex? Should Society Be Concerned About Teen Sex? How Should Society Respond to Teen Sex? What Should Teens Be Taught About Sex? The consequences of teen sexual activity can be high, as evidenced by U.S. pregnancy and STD rates. As experts debate how best to prevent such consequences, comparisons between the United States and the rest of the world can be useful.

CHAPTER 1

What Factors Influence Teen Attitudes Toward Sex?

Chapter Preface

Teens are exposed to countless sexual references in the music they listen to, the magazines they read, and the television shows and movies they watch. Idealistic 1950s and 1960s television shows like *Leave It to Beaver* and *The Brady Bunch*, where a kiss was nearly taboo, have been replaced by *Dawson's Creek* and *One Tree Hill*, where teen pregnancy, birth control, homosexuality, and sex are integral themes in many of the episodes. An ongoing debate rages about whether sex on TV influences teens' sexual behavior and if so, to what extent. A number of studies done since 2000 indicate that sexy television programs do impact, both negatively and positively, the ways teens think about sex. Television shows have long been a focus of study for many experts exploring the factors that shape teen sexual attitudes.

Statistics help explain why television has so much influence on teen attitudes about sex. According to the Campaign for a Commercial-Free Childhood, 83 percent of episodes of the top twenty shows among teen viewers in 2003 contained some sexual content, including 20 percent with sexual intercourse. It also found that girls who watched more than fourteen hours of rap music videos per week were more likely to have multiple sex partners and to be diagnosed with a sexually transmitted disease.

Moreover, the Committee on Public Education reports that teens spend more time watching TV than they do in school or with their parents. The average eighteen-year-old has spent about fifteen thousand hours watching television. The committee also found:

- About 66 percent of prime time shows contain some sexual content.
- Sixty-two percent of individual scenes in TV programs included sexual behavior, and 28 percent of these scenes placed the primary emphasis on sex.
- Each new season, television programs contain more sexual content than the previous year.

Another way to examine how TV influences teens' sexual attitudes is to look at how experts rate the shows. Every year, the Parents Television Council (PTC) rates the best and worst shows on prime-time television on ABC, CBS, Fox, NBC, PAX, UPN, and the WB. For the 2003–2004 season, the two worst show were aimed directly at teens: *Everwood* and *That '70s Show*. The council said of the number one worst show, "*Everwood* gives every appearance of being a family drama but it's nothing of the kind. What makes *Everwood* problematic is the careless and irresponsible treatment of sexual issues, especially when the teenage characters are involved. . . . *Everwood*'s reckless messages about sex without consequences are expressly targeted to impressionable teens." Other teen shows rated by PTC as among the worst due primarily to their treatment of teen sex include *Dawson's Creek, Buffy the Vampire Slayer, Angel*, and nearly everything on MTV.

In contrast, the PTC cites several teen-oriented shows as being among the best on television, often for their realistic portrayals of the negative consequences of teen sex. These include *7th Heaven, Roswell, Smallville, Boy Meets World*, and *Sabrina, the Teenage Witch*.

Despite such ratings, there is no clear consensus on what is bad and what is good for teens to watch. For example, the popular NBC sitcom *Friends* aired its controversial "condom episode" in 2003. During the episode, the character Rachel reveals that she is pregnant even though another character, Ross, used a condom while having sex with her. The episode was praised in a Kaiser Family Foundation study for giving specific information about the effectiveness of condoms, noting that they work about 95 percent of the time. "The possibility of condom failure and the resulting consequence of pregnancy were thus vividly communicated to a very large adolescent audience, as was the message that condoms almost always work," the study stated. Yet the PTC cited that episode as one reason why it ranked *Friends* as one of the ten worst shows on TV.

Television is but one of the many influences on teen sexual attitudes. The authors in the following chapter explore other factors that shape teens' views. In order to reduce sexually transmitted diseases and pregnancy rates among teens, it is crucial to understand how sexual attitudes are formed.

"While most mothers disapprove of their sons or daughters being sexually active, their kids don't always get the message."

Parents Influence Teen Attitudes Toward Sex

Robert W. Blum

Robert W. Blum is a physician and lecturer with the University of Minnesota Office of Pediatrics and Adolescent Health. In the following viewpoint he discusses two studies finding that parents, mothers in particular, have an important influence on their teenagers' sexual activity. Blum reports that the more involved parents are with their teens and the higher the level of closeness between parents and teens, the less likely teens are to engage in sexual intercourse.

As you read this, consider the following questions:

1. According to the author, research on parent-teen relationships vary, depending on what?
2. Were most parents who responded to the National Longitudinal Study of Adolescent Health fathers or mothers, according to Blum?
3. When teens perceive that their mother disapproves of them having sex, according to the author, are they less or more likely to delay having sex?

Robert W. Blum, *Mothers' Influence on Teen Sex: Connections That Promote Postponing Sexual Intercourse*. Minneapolis, MN: Center for Adolescent Health and Development, 2002. Copyright © 2002 by Robert W. Blum. Reproduced by permission.

P arents matter. The values and beliefs we share with our
kids matter. Our actions as role models matter. How we
relate to our children matters. Or at least we believe that it
does.

From a research perspective, most of what we know and
believe is based on cross-sectional data. Cross-sectional data
can show us relationships or associations where they exist
but they can't tell us what causes the relationship. Longitudinal research is necessary to understand the sequence of influences in a relationship—to better understand causality.

As Brent Miller found in his review commissioned by the
National Campaign to Prevent Teen Pregnancy (1998),
cross-sectional research on sexual decision-making among
teens suggests some important parent, family, and environ-
mental factors:

- Parent/child connectedness (support, closeness, warmth)
  is associated with an older age of first intercourse and a
  lower frequency of sex during adolescence.
- Parent attitudes and values disapproving of adolescent
  sexual intercourse (or unprotected intercourse) is associated with later age of sexual initiation.
- Living in disorganized or dangerous neighborhoods and/
  or in poverty, living with a single parent, and having been
  a victim of sexual abuse, and having siblings who are sexually active, pregnant or parenting are all associated with
  increased risk of an adolescent initiating sex at a younger
  age.
- Biologic and inherited factors such as hormonal levels
  and timing of puberty are associated with timing of first
  sexual intercourse.
- The research is less clear as to the role of parental su-
  pervision/regulation. Some studies suggest it is associated with a delay in the onset of intercourse while other
  studies show that strict parenting is associated with a
  higher risk of early sexual initiation.
- It is uncertain to what extent and how parent/teen communication about sex and contraception affects adolescent sexual behaviors. A number of studies show that
  open communication about sex is associated with later
  sexual initiation and/or higher contraceptive use, while

an equal number show no association between communication and pregnancy risk and a few studies even show an increased risk of early sexual initiation with open parent/teen communication.

Research findings on parent-teen relationships vary depending on who is asked the questions—parents or teens. Overall, agreement between parents and teens tends to be low on how much they talk together about sex. In a study by James Jaccard and his colleagues, mothers tended to underestimate their teens' sexual behavior and teens tended to underestimate their mothers' level of disapproval of their engaging in sexual activity.

Recently, Jaccard and his colleague Patricia Dittus published longitudinal research from the National Longitudinal Study of Adolescent Health (Add Health). They found:

- Teens who reported more satisfaction in their relationship with their mother were less likely to report having sex in the subsequent year, more likely to use birth control the last time they had sex and less likely to get pregnant.
- The more disapproving adolescents perceived their mother to be toward their engaging in sexual intercourse, the less likely they were to have sexual intercourse.
- Teens' perceptions of their mothers' attitudes toward abstinence are more predictive of sexual outcomes (e.g., intercourse, use of birth control, pregnancy) than actual maternal attitudes.

This monograph delves further into the Add Health Study to better understand mother-teen relationships as they affect sexual behavior among teens who are not yet sexually active. What is it specifically about those relationships that make a difference and for which teenagers? In this report we look at several questions:

- Are teens aware of their mothers' disapproval of their having sex?
- Do mothers know whether their teens have had sex?
- Do mothers talk to their teens about sex and birth control? What influence does it have?
- Mothers talk, teens' perceptions: What matters?
- What effect do closeness and connectedness have on teen sex?

- What else about mothers make a difference for sexual initiation? . . .

This monograph reports research on how mothers influence their teens' decisions about when to have sex. That is not because fathers are not important. Much to the contrary. Rather, nearly all parents who responded to the Add Health interview were mothers. It is also important to note that previous research has suggested that the influence of mothers outweighs that of fathers as it relates to the sexual behaviors of their teenage sons and daughters. Thus, a better understanding of how mothers' influence works is an important step in preventing negative sexual health outcomes among teens.

While most mothers disapprove of their sons or daughters being sexually active, their kids don't always get the message. And there are differences among boys and girls. Specifically, when mom strongly disapproves, 30% of girls do not believe they do. For boys, nearly half do not believe mom disapproves of their having sex when mothers tell us that they do.

It is clear that what mothers believe is not consistently getting through to their teenagers.

The Add Health data allowed the researchers to look at mothers' awareness of their teens' sex lives. When teenagers reported that they had not had sexual intercourse, mothers were almost always correct in their assessment (more than 97% accurate). The opposite, however, is not so true. . . . When teens tell us that they have had sexual intercourse, mothers have about a 50–50 chance of being right in their assessment.

Most mothers say they talk to their children about sex. In fact, in both Add Health studies nearly all mothers of teenagers who have not yet had intercourse say that they talk to their children about issues such as birth control and the potential consequences of having sex at least to some extent. Mothers in the study of 14–15-year-olds indicate that although they feel more uncomfortable speaking with their daughters than with their sons about sex, they are slightly more likely to actually talk with daughters about sex and birth control. Specifically, just under half (48%) of mothers say they discuss sex and birth control with their sons at least "a moderate amount" or "a great deal"; and just over half of mothers (52%) say they discuss sex and birth control with their daughters to a similar extent. While there is not a lot of difference in the amount of talk mothers report with sons and daughters, mothers are much more likely to say that they recommended a specific form of birth control to their 14–15-year-old sons than to their daughters. Specifically, 35% of mothers said they had recommended a specific birth control method to their sons compared with 22% for their daughters.

Gamble. © 1991 by *The Florida Times-Union*, King Features Syndicate. Reproduced by permission of Ed Gamble.

Whether mothers feel uncomfortable with discussing sex did not have any impact on whether either 14–15-year-old males or females initiated sexual intercourse during the one-year study period; neither did how much mothers report that they discussed sex or birth control influence transition to first intercourse for their sons or daughters.

When mothers in the 8th–11th grade study reported having recommended a specific form of birth control, their adolescent children were slightly less likely to perceive that their mother disapproved of them having sex. When mothers spoke with their teens about the negative consequences of sex, such as problems that come from early pregnancy and the cost to a teen's reputation, it had no impact on initiating intercourse for either boys or girls.

As noted earlier, most of what mothers' report that they believe and say about teen sex has little direct impact on their teenagers transitioning to first intercourse. Rather, mothers' report of strong disapproval appears to have an effect only when teens accurately perceive that disapproval. When teens perceive that their mother strongly disapproves of them having sex, they are more likely to delay initial sexual intercourse.

This effect was seen for both 8th and 9th graders and 10th and 11th graders. Although, as a group, teens tend to underestimate their mothers' disapproval of them having sex, teens are significantly more likely to perceive disapproval when there is actual disapproval. However, that is not always the case. . . .

Teen perceptions are shaped by more than what mother says. For younger teens, connectedness influences perceptions. When 8th and 9th graders feel connected to mom, they are nearly half again as likely to perceive mothers' disapproval. This effect was not seen for older teens. On the other hand, in the study of 8th–11th graders, when mothers recommended birth control to their adolescent, teens were slightly less likely to perceive mothers' disapproval.

One study measures parent-teen satisfaction from the mother's perspective; the other study measures connectedness as reported by teens. When mothers report feeling satisfied with their relationship with their 14–15-year-old daughters, their daughters were less likely to report having had sexual intercourse. Mothers' reported satisfaction with their relationships with their sons, on the other hand, had no impact on the timing of first intercourse.

We use the term connectedness to describe the teens' view of the relationship with his or her mother. By connectedness, we mean how close teens feel to their mothers, how much they feel mother cares about them, how warm and loving mother is, how good communication is with their mother and how satisfied teens feel with their relationship with their mother.

Connectedness is not the same as mothers' satisfaction with their relationships with their teenage sons or daughters.

The protective power of connectedness appears to be related to adolescents' gender and age. While high levels of mother-child connectedness are independently related to delays in first sexual intercourse among 8th and 9th grade boys and girls and among 10th and 11th grade boys, the protective effect of connectedness appears to diminish for older girls. High levels of mother-teen connectedness were not significantly associated with delays in sexual intercourse among 10th and 11th grade girls.

Percent of Adolescents Who Accurately Perceive Their Mothers' Level of Disapproval of Sex

Girls	Mothers' Level of Disapproval	
Do Adolescents Accurately Perceive Mothers' Level of Disapproval?	Strong Disapproval	Less than Strong Disapproval
Yes	70%	56%
No	30%	44%

Boys	Mothers' Level of Disapproval	
Do Adolescents Accurately Perceive Mothers' Level of Disapproval?	Strong Disapproval	Less than Strong Disapproval
Yes	54%	71%
No	45%	29%

Robert W. Blum, *Mothers' Influence on Teen Sex: Connections That Promote Postponing Sexual Intercourse.* Minneapolis, MN: Center for Adolescent Health and Development, 2002.

Mothers appear to slow the progression from teens' romantic involvement to first intercourse in several ways. Add Health findings suggest that girls who have mothers with higher levels of education are less likely to transition to intercourse at every age studied. On the other hand, teens who had mothers who were highly religious were no less likely than other teens over the one-year study period to start having intercourse.

Being actively engaged in the lives of their daughters is

another way mothers may help to delay early intercourse. Mothers who report frequently talking with the parents of their daughters' friends had daughters who were less likely to have initiated intercourse over the one-year study period. None of these findings held true for boys.

This study, like others before, suggests that mothers have less influence on the timing of first sexual intercourse among their sons than among their daughters. For adolescent boys, other social influences—such as those provided by fathers, siblings or peers—may outweigh maternal influences on the timing of first sexual intercourse.

- When it comes to delaying the initiation of sexual intercourse, caring and connectedness are important—especially for younger teens.
- Simply stating parents' disapproval of teen sex is not enough. Clearly, some teenagers do not get the message. We do not know exactly why. Perhaps parents are not consistent in what they say. Maybe it is because we do not really start talking to our teens about these issues until we believe that they are in a serious relationship. When they do get the message, teens are more likely to delay sexual intercourse.
- While so much is made these days over what we should say to our kids about sex, the present research suggests that other aspects of parenting may have a greater influence, such as knowing our kids' friends and their friends' parents. Other factors that may make a difference include: having high expectations for school, having rules and regulations, knowing where one's child is and having meals together.
- About 50% of parents seem to be unaware that their sons and daughters have started to have sex. If we are to be successful in providing our children guidance, perhaps we need to be more aware of what is going on in their lives.
- Despite the fact that mothers are slightly more likely to discuss sex with their daughters than with their sons, they are much less likely to suggest birth control to their daughters. Rather, more mother-daughter discussions appear to focus on the risks of early sex—suggest-

ing perhaps that, like society as a whole, mothers may be more oriented to influencing their daughters' sexual behavior and more oriented to influencing their son's risk of infection and early parenting.

- As much as we wish otherwise, these research findings, as well as those of others, show that there are no simple answers for parents when it comes to talking to kids about birth control. [One study] found that teens whose parents recommended contraception were more likely to have intercourse. The present study, while showing that parent recommendations of contraception diminish teen perceptions of maternal disapproval, showed that such recommendations were not associated with a greater likelihood of teen sex. The differences in the two studies may be the result of sample size or methods used. [The study] also found that teens whose parents recommended contraception were more likely to use it. For each of the studies, the findings are statistically significant but the effects are not large.

This leaves parents with a mixed message. While a recommendation of birth control by parents may be associated with increased use, there is also the risk that it may be misconstrued by teens as sanctioning early sex when that is not the intent. To the extent that our messages, values and behaviors as parents are more consistent, teens may be able to comprehend both what we believe and what we say.

There is no single litmus test for parenting. While we need to keep our teenagers safe, our goal is broader than keeping teens "problem-free."

Our goals are to raise teens who are socially, physically, morally and emotionally healthy. In addition to promoting health, we want to aid our teenagers in acquiring the academic, social, vocational and civic competencies, as well as the confidence and character they will need to become capable, engaged and caring adults. Keeping them safe from the consequences of early sex or even from early sex itself is but one step to this much larger goal.

"One of your greatest challenges will be dealing with peer pressure. To stand up for what you believe in when others are doing the opposite takes great strength."

Peer Pressure Shapes Teen Attitudes About Sex

Michael J. Basso

Michael J. Basso taught health and sexuality in a Miami school for eight years. He is currently a health scientist and public health advisor for the Centers for Disease Control and Prevention in Atlanta. Basso argues in this viewpoint that teens are under tremendous pressure from their peers to have sex. However, he claims that many teens successfully deal with such pressure and avoid sexual intercourse. He suggests that teens practice ways of saying "no" to sex.

As you read, consider the following questions:
1. What percentage of the author's teen students report that they are actually having sex, according to Basso?
2. How can teens say no to someone who is pressuring them to have sex, as explained by the author?
3. What is peer pressure, as defined by Basso?

Michael J. Basso, "How to Say No to Sex," *The Underground Guide to Teenage Sexuality*. Minneapolis, MN: Fairview Press, 2003. Copyright © 2003 by Michael J. Basso. All rights reserved. Reproduced by permission.

You are a special person with your own thoughts, feelings, and beliefs. Throughout your life you will be challenged to defend what you think, feel, and believe. Sometimes this battle will be easy, but most of the time the pressure to conform, be like "everyone else," or do what someone else wants you to do is difficult to overcome.

As more and more pressure is put on you to forget about what you think, feel, or believe, you will be tempted to take the easy way out and give up on your beliefs to make another person "happy" or just to stop her/him from pressuring you.

We have all been pressured into doing something we didn't really want to do. Almost always, we felt embarrassed, ashamed, and angry at ourselves because of it. The trick to becoming successful in life is to learn from our mistakes and, most important, to learn from other people's mistakes.

If you can learn from another person's mistakes, you will be able to avoid a lot of headaches in your own life. Unfortunately, millions of young people each year learn the hard way about teenage pregnancy and [sexually transmitted diseases (STDs)] because they refuse to learn from other people's mistakes. . . .

Contrary to popular belief, not all teens are having sex. In fact, in surveys I give my fifteen- and sixteen-year-old students who live under some of the harshest conditions in America, only about 35 percent of the females have had sex, which means that 65 percent have not. Interestingly, of the 35 percent who had sex, 90 percent said they regretted it and wish they had waited.

Now, before you think my young ladies are lying, you should know that the surveys are anonymous (no names) and are completed in a way that no one can see what the next person is writing. Each year, just about the same results show up.

The guys are different. About 60 percent of my fifteen- and sixteen-year-old males report that they have had sex (40 percent have not). These percentages are pretty close to results from similar surveys given around the nation. Not everyone is having sex!

More important than what other people do is what you are going to do. Do you want to avoid an unplanned pregnancy?

Do you want to avoid becoming infected with an STD (including HIV/AIDS)? Would you rather postpone intercourse until you're older? If you answered yes to these questions, you and millions of other teens just like you should take pride in who you are and learn how to defend and protect your thoughts, feelings, and beliefs. You can do it! You will be happy you did.

Plan for High-Pressure Situations

Before you get into a high-pressure situation, you should do the following:

Plan ahead. Know where you are going and what you will be doing before you go out.

Look for signs of a possible problem. There are a few things that can lead to a problem situation. Beer, wine coolers, alcohol, marijuana, or other drugs being bought or used may lead to trouble.

Avoid "hot spots," places where there are no people around (such as a house where no adult is home or empty parks/beaches at night).

Know how to communicate your feelings. Practice assertive communication and body language, using "put off" words and moves (actions that get you out of the situation). Each of these communication skills should be practiced until you know them like your ABCs. Go somewhere by yourself and practice verbal messages and "put off" lines until there are at least two or three that you say very well. You will probably feel stupid standing in a room talking to yourself, but after memorizing and saying each line ten or twenty times, it gets easier to do. You may think, "I don't need to do this" or "When the time comes, I'll be ready." This would be a big mistake. When you're in a high-pressure situation, your mind tends to freeze up and you don't usually think very clearly. Let's not forget you're in the middle of a heart-and-mind battleground.

Once you get good at repeating what you really want to say, try it in front of a mirror. Then make it more difficult by adding body language. Make believe you are your favorite actor/actress acting in a big movie.

Here are descriptions and a few tips for each communication skill you should practice.

Learn "Put Off" Moves

Verbal messages are any spoken words that say what you feel or think. Repeat verbal messages if necessary. After giving a verbal message, you could ask, "Do you hear me?" or "Do you understand me?" You do not have to explain why you do not want to have sex. "No" is good enough.

More important, when you say no verbally you must also say no with your body. Body language is what your body says through facial expressions, hand gestures, how close you sit/stand next to someone, or any body movement or stance. Gestures and expressions are forms of body language. Your body language should match your verbal message.

"Put off" moves are any words or actions that interrupt what the other person is saying and doing. These moves give you a chance to get out of the situation, giving you time to think, leave, or calm down. Examples of "put off" moves are:

- "Not now. Let's go somewhere."
- "I have to go."
- "Not tonight. I feel like I'm going to be sick."
- "I have to call home."
- "I have to go to the bathroom."

If you want to be successful in doing what you believe is best for you, practice your communication skills. It's like having a big test at school; study until you know the material backward and forward. You will still feel emotional pressure, but if you know your lines, this will help ease some of the pressure on you to have sex. . . .

Communicate Your Feelings

Any person who tries to get you to do something you don't feel is right is someone you should avoid being around.

If your girlfriend/boyfriend is one of these people who seems to ignore what you say and makes excuses for pressuring you, it may be time to trade up and find someone who is more sensitive to who you are and what you're about. Try communicating your feelings again. Perhaps there was some miscommunication or misunderstanding. If your partner continues with the pressure, it's clear she/he is only interested in getting what she/he wants and doesn't really care about who you are, what you're about, and what you feel.

It's difficult being your own person and doing what you know is right, but the more you stand up for yourself and defend what you believe in, the stronger you become as a person. The stronger you become as a person, the easier it is for you to defend your beliefs and do what is right for you.

When you start to feel the pressure, say no quickly, without even thinking. The sooner you say no, and the more often you say no, the easier it becomes to say no. Don't give in to the pressure and say yes just to make the other person happy; you will probably regret it. . . .

What Is Peer Pressure?

Peer pressure is when friends or people around your own age say or do things to get you to do something you may not really want to do.

An example would be a group of friends or "peers" standing around smoking cigarettes. In this case, they would be doing something that might put pressure on you to try smoking. If this same group of people said to you, "How about a cigarette? C'mon, try it. It's no big deal!" then they would be saying something to pressure you into what you may not really want to do.

Peer pressure is another part of growing up that all people face. Sometimes to try and fit in with a group of people, you may be tempted to do things you don't really want to do. You will be faced with this challenge over and over again.

An example of sexual peer pressure might be standing at a party and listening to a group of males or females talk about how they "went all the way" (had sex) with their boyfriends or girlfriends. They might then say to you, "When was the last time you had sex?" or "When are you going to have sex?" or "What's wrong with you?" This is classic peer pressure.

Peer pressure usually makes you feel uneasy, uncomfortable, or like something is wrong. You may feel worried, unhappy, angry, or confused. This is because you may know what is best for you, but your peers are gently trying to get you to do what they want you to do. You certainly want to be friendly with other people or be part of the crowd, so you're tempted to give up on what you know is best for you and do what your peers are saying or doing.

Be Your Own Person

One of your greatest challenges will be dealing with peer pressure. To stand up for what you believe in when others are doing the opposite takes great strength. Some people handle peer pressure well, and others not well at all. Get into the habit of standing up for yourself. The more success you have early on, the easier it is to stay successful. Tell people how you feel early in the conversation. This will usually discourage most people from putting any pressure on you. Speak up!

The Role of Peers on Sexual Decisions

The peer group is an important factor in adolescent development and has some bearing on teenagers' decisions about sex.

- Adolescents (ages 13 to 18) report that they are most likely to get information about sexual health issues from their peers.
- Pressure to engage in sex increases during middle adolescence. Peer group attitudes about sex influence the attitudes and behaviors of teenagers.

Youths who resist engaging in sexual activity tend to have friends who are abstinent as well. They also tend to have strong personal beliefs in abstinence and the perception of negative parental reactions. Youths who are sexually active tend to believe that most of their friends are sexually active as well, that rewards outweigh the costs of sexual involvement, that sex overall is rewarding, and that it is all right for unmarried adolescents over age 16 to engage in intercourse.

Sheila Clark, "Parents, Peers, and Pressures: Identifying the Influences on Responsible Sexual Decision-Making," 2002. www.naswdc.org.

If you have not been very successful in dealing with peer pressure in the past, remind yourself that this time you're a new person. If you're faced with a high-pressure situation, treat it as an opportunity to be successful. You will be what you act like. Be your own person—strong, confident, and ready to do what needs to be done. Avoid people who pressure you. Would a real friend pressure you to do something you didn't want to do? Would a real friend pressure you to do something that would be harmful? Friends come and go. The consequences of drugs, STDs, and unplanned pregnancy can stay with you for a lifetime.

Avoid high-pressure situations if you don't handle peer pressure very well. Places like parties, for example, can be fun, but if there are people there using drugs, having sex, or doing things you do not want to be a part of, you will feel better off choosing to go somewhere else. Otherwise, have a plan to be your own person.

Get help from parents and teachers if you're confused. Parents and teachers have gone through the same things you're going through now. Often, they are able to help you and support you. Just ask!

Dealing with Peer Pressure

What if my friends bother me to have sex with my partner? This has been going on for a long time and can be considered just one of the many types of peer pressure that teens experience while growing up. Like any other kind of pressure/harassment, it can make you feel uncomfortable.

One way of dealing with peer pressure effectively is to tell the person pressuring you how you feel (or to back off) as soon as he/she starts bothering you. If the pressure is starting to annoy you, simply say (using verbal language and matching body language) that you don't want to be bothered with his/her comments. Here are a few quick comments you may be able to use, to be accompanied by a serious expression on your face:

- "Hey, we're good friends, so I know you won't take this the wrong way, but. . . ."
- "Lighten up about this sex thing."
- "My business is my business, not yours."
- "Don't worry so much about what my boyfriend/girlfriend and I do. We're doing just fine."
- "You need to get a life of your own instead of poking around in mine so much."

These comments are a bit aggressive, and most experts will say to use "I" statements like, "I don't like when you ask me personal questions about my romantic life," which can be effective with some people. However, you know and I know that most teens don't speak in such rational terms. Even so, some people just don't seem to get the idea unless you spell it out for them. Sometimes a comment that is quick and to the point can be as effective as an "I" statement.

Part of the fun in going out with someone is being able to talk to your friends about the fun places you go and the fun things you do with your boyfriend/girlfriend. Whether or not you have sex with your boyfriend/girlfriend is not something that should be shared with your friends unless you and your partner agree on it. You may be tempted to share every detail about your romantic life, but this usually makes things messy. By sharing intimate moments or feelings that your partner may not want other people to know about, you may betray the trust your boyfriend/girlfriend has in you. You might also add fuel to the fire by getting your friends all worked up about your relationship. It's usually best to keep the private things private between you and your boyfriend/girlfriend. . . .

You can express your feelings without giving up on your beliefs or giving in to another person. The decision to stand up for what you believe in and do the things you know are right takes courage. Many people just go along with what other people are doing or what other people want. Being an individual, being strong, means being able to resist the pressure to give up on yourself and your values. You can be your own person.

"When asked where they have learned the most about sex, younger adolescents (13–15 years old) rank the mass media fourth behind parents, friends, and schools. Older adolescents (16–17 years old) put friends first, then parents, and then the media."

The Mass Media Influence Teen Sexual Attitudes

Jane D. Brown

Jane D. Brown is a professor at the University of North Carolina School of Journalism and Mass Communication in Chapel Hill. Her research focuses on how adolescents' health is affected by the mass media and how the media can help adolescents live healthier lives. In this viewpoint she argues that the mass media is becoming an increasingly important way for teens to learn about sex. She also examines the increase of sexual content directed at teens in television, movies, music, and the Internet. Although more research is needed on the connection between sex in the media and teen sexual attitudes, according to Brown studies suggest that pervasive media portrayals of sex encourage young people to engage in sexual activity.

As you read, consider the following questions:
1. What is the most popular word used in Internet searches, according to Brown?
2. In the author's view, how did the media cover AIDS when it was first discovered?
3. What is missing from the media's portrayals of sex, in Brown's opinion?

Jane D. Brown, "Mass Media Influences on Sexuality," *Journal of Sex Research*, vol. 39, February 2002, pp. 42–45. Copyright © 2002 by the Society for the Scientific Study of Sexuality, Inc. Reproduced by permission.

The mass media are an increasingly accessible way for people to learn about and see sexual behavior. The media may be especially important for young people as they are developing their own sexual beliefs and patterns of behavior, and as parents and schools remain reluctant to discuss sexual topics.

In the United States, young people spend 6 to 7 hours each day on average with some form of media. A national survey in 1999 found that one third of young children (2 to 7 years old) and two thirds of older children and adolescents (8 to 18 years old) have a television in their own bedroom. Many of those televisions also are hooked up to cable and a Videocassette Recorder (VCR).

Sexual talk and displays are increasingly frequent and explicit in this mediated world. One content analysis found that sexual content that ranged from flirting to sexual intercourse had increased from slightly more than half of television programs in 1997–1998 to more than two-thirds of the programs in the 1999–2000 season. Depiction of intercourse (suggestive or explicit) occurred in one of every 10 programs.

One fifth to one half of music videos, depending on the music genre (e.g., country, rock, rap) portray sexuality or eroticism. Two thirds of Hollywood movies made each year are R-rated; most young people have seen these movies long before they are the required 16 years old. Although teen girls' and women's magazines, such as *Seventeen* and *Glamour* have increased their coverage of sexual health issues over the past decade, the majority of advertising and editorial content in these magazines remains focused on what girls and women should do to get and keep their man.

Gay, lesbian, bisexual, and transgender youth rarely find themselves represented in the mainstream media. Although a few of the youth-targeted programs such as "Dawson's Creek" and "Will and Grace" have included gay characters, what some have called compulsory heterosexuality prevails.

The Internet has increased dramatically the availability of sexually explicit content. Computer and Internet use is diffusing more rapidly than any previous technology; as of the end of 1999, more than half (56%) of all adults in the United

States were online. It is expected that by 2010 most U.S. homes with children will have access to the Internet.

The Internet and Pornography

The word sex is the most popular search term used on the Internet today. The Internet may have both positive and negative effects on sexual health. According to one national survey of young people (10–17 years old) who regularly used the Internet, one out of four said he or she had encountered unwanted pornography in the past year, and one out of five had been exposed to unwanted sexual solicitations or approaches. At the same time, a number of sites, such as the American Social Health Association's iwannaknow.org, promote healthy sexual behavior and provide young people with advice on communication in relationships as well as methods for protecting against sexually transmitted diseases.

Despite increasing public concern about the potential health risks of early, unprotected sexual activity, most of the mass media rarely depict the three C's of responsible sexual behavior: Commitment, Contraceptives, and consideration of Consequences. Although more than half of the couples who engage in sexual intercourse on television are in an established relationship, 1 in 10 are couples who have met only recently; one quarter do not maintain a relationship after having sex.

Only about 1 in 10 of the programs on television that include sexual content mentions the possible consequences or the need to use contraceptives or protection against [sexually transmitted diseases (STDs)]. Unintended pregnancies rarely are shown as the outcome of unprotected sex, and STDs other than HIV/AIDS are almost never discussed. Abortion is a taboo topic, too controversial for commercial television and magazines.

Do audiences learn about sex from this array of sexual information and portrayals? The perceived sensitivity of sex as a research topic and a focus on television to the exclusion of other media unfortunately has restricted the kind of research that has been done. Much of the empirical work has been analyses of content that allow only speculation about what effects the content might have on audiences. But an emerging set of studies that go beyond content to address how audiences select, interpret, and apply sexual content suggests that the media may play an important role, especially for young people.

The Media Are a Top Source for Sex Information

When asked where they have learned the most about sex, younger adolescents (13–15 years old) rank the mass media fourth behind parents, friends, and schools. Older adolescents (16–17 years old) put friends first, then parents, and then the media. More than half of the high school boys and girls in a national survey in 1997 said they had learned about birth control, contraception, or preventing pregnancy from television; almost two thirds (63%) of the girls (and 40% of the boys) said they had learned about these topics from magazines.

The media are used as sources of information about sexuality at some times more than others. One qualitative study found three patterns of sexual media use among early adolescent girls (11–15 years old) that suggested that sexual portrayals in the media were attended to more when girls were interested personally in learning about relationship norms, strategies for establishing relationships, and tips on how to get sexually attractive. Some girls still found depictions of sex in the media (e.g., nudity in advertisements) "gross" and "disgusting," while other girls had papered their walls with images of media models they lusted after or aspired to be. Still other girls, typically those who had been involved in sexual relationships, were less enamored with the mainstream media's sexual fantasy and had turned to "oppositional" media (e.g., fringe music groups, teen-produced magazines, aka 'zines) that spoke more to the kinds of relationships they wanted.

We know that patterns of media use differ dramatically by age, gender, race/ethnicity, and socioeconomic level. Girls and women typically choose softer music, and more relationship-oriented television programs, movies, and magazines, while boys and men prefer more action and activity-oriented media and sports programming, heavier rock and rap music, action and adventure movies, music, and sports magazines. African Americans typically view more television than Whites, prefer television programming and movies that feature Black characters, and listen to different genres of music. Thus, it is important to consider the media's effects on sexuality within subgroups: All people will not be seeing the same set of sexual messages—some will see much more than others, some will be seeking out the sexual content, some will try not to be exposed to it.

All members of an audience also will not see or interpret the same messages in the same way. One striking example of differences in interpretation was found in an analysis of one of rock star Madonna's early music videos, "Papa Don't Preach." When first released, newspaper columnist Ellen Goodman called it "a commercial for teenage pregnancy," while the religious right said it was a stand against abortion. College students who saw the video differed in their "reading" of the video, too. Although most White females thought the video was about a teen girl deciding to keep her unborn child ("baby"), Black males were more likely to think the girl (Madonna) in the video was singing about wanting to keep her boyfriend "baby." Since the young men were identifying primarily with the dilemma of the boyfriend in the video, they were less likely than the female viewers to see or hear the cues that suggested pregnancy.

Other studies also conclude that young males and females interpret media content differently [and] . . . have shown college students portions of situation comedies such as "Roseanne" and "Martin." They find that young women are more likely than young men to think the sexual scenes they see are realistic, and the women are more approving than the men of behaviors that are relationship-maintaining (e.g., jealous husband protecting wife) and less approving of relationship threats (e.g., man contemplating cheating).

The Effects of Media on Teen Sex Behavior

As people attend to and interpret sexual media content, they also evaluate and may or may not incorporate what they are seeing in their own developing sense of sexuality. This is the step that we traditionally have thought of as media effects. Does the sexual content in the media influence how people behave sexually? Are people having sex earlier, with more partners, without protection or affection because of what they see in the media?

The answer to these questions is a qualified "yes." Qualified, because even though we know a fair amount about the ubiquity of sexual content in the media, we still have only sparse research on the effects of sexual media content. According to classic social scientific methods, an ideal test of the effects of sexual media content would involve either randomized assignment to different sexual media diets, or longitudinal surveys. Such studies would establish whether media exposure or behavior came first, and would allow for generalizations about what kinds of media content cause what kinds of behaviors.

Teens, TV, and Music Videos

The average teenager spends 3 to 4 hours per day watching television.

For every hour of programming watched by adolescents, an average of 6.7 scenes included sexual topics and about 10% of scenes portray couples engaging in sexual intercourse. One-third of shows with sexual content involve teen characters. . . .

Adolescents exposed to TV with sexual content are more likely than other adolescents to:

• Overestimate the frequency of some sexual behaviors

• Have more permissive attitudes toward premarital sex

• Think that having sex is beneficial.

S. Liliana Escobar-Chavez et al. "Impact of the Media on Adolescent Sexual Attitudes and Behaviors." Centers for Disease Control and Prevention Report, January 30, 2004. www.cdc.gov.

The relatively few correlational and still fewer experimental studies of the relationship between exposure to sexual media content and effects suggest that the media do have an impact in at least three ways: (a) by keeping sexual behavior on public and personal agendas, (b) by reinforcing a relatively consistent set of sexual and relationship norms, and (c) by rarely including sexually responsible models. Three theoretical perspectives often used by communication researchers: (a) Agenda Setting/Framing, (b) Cultivation, and (c) Cognitive Social Learning Theory, help to explain why we expect these outcomes.

Agenda Setting and Framing Theories propose that the media tell people both what is important in the world around them, and how to think about the events and people who inhabit that world. Although rarely thought of as sex educators, even the news media help keep sexual behavior salient. The American public and policy makers frequently are faced with news stories about abandoned babies, sex-enhancing drugs, and even presidential sexual affairs. Topics and images that are frequent and prominent in the media become topics that audiences think are important.

Early coverage of the AIDS epidemic provides a good example of how agenda setting and framing work in relation to a sexual health issue. When AIDS was first discovered, the media were slow to cover the story because it was considered a problem only for gay men, intravenous drug users, and a few Hemophiliacs. It took a number of years and the deaths of celebrities such as Rock Hudson for the media to put the problem higher on the news agenda, and even longer for the frame to shift from one of a problem of morality to one of a threat to the public's health.

The media are in a unique position to get people thinking and talking about specific issues, while keeping other issues from the public eye. The people who are cited or figure prominently in the stories become known as the heroes or the villains, while some solutions and not others are offered. People use the stories they see both in the news and in entertainment media as reference points about what's important and to compare what they already know, or think they know about what's good and bad, and what should be done about problems. The result often reinforces stereotypes and helps define what is considered appropriate and inappropriate behavior in the culture.

Television Distorts Teen Sex Concepts

According to Cultivation Theory, television is the most powerful storyteller in the culture, one that continually repeats the myths and ideologies, the facts and patterns of relationships that define and legitimize the social order. According to the cultivation hypothesis, a steady dose of television, over time, acts like the pull of gravity toward an imagined center.

This pull results in a shared set of conceptions and expectations about reality among otherwise diverse viewers.

Tests of the hypothesis have found, for example, that junior and senior high school students who frequently viewed daytime soap operas were more likely than those who watched less often to believe that single mothers have relatively easy lives, have good jobs, and do not live in poverty. Exposure to stereotypical images of gender and sexuality in music videos has been found to increase older adolescents' acceptance of nonmarital sexual behavior and interpersonal violence. Heavier television viewers also have been found to have more negative attitudes toward remaining a virgin.

Others have shown that prolonged exposure to erotica leads to exaggerated estimates of the prevalence of more unusual kinds of sexual activity (e.g., group sex, sadomasochistic practices, bestiality), less expectation of sexual exclusivity with partners, and apprehension that sexual inactivity constitutes a health risk. In one experimental study, college students who were exposed to about 5 hours of sexually explicit films over 6 weeks were more likely than a control group to express increased callousness toward women and trivialize rape as a criminal offense.

Two correlational studies have found relationships between the frequency of television viewing and initiation of intercourse in samples of high school students. However, because these were only cross-sectional analyses, it was not possible to say with certainty which came first—the TV viewing or the sexual behavior. It is possible that teens who were becoming interested in sex had turned to sexual content in the media because it was now salient in their lives. It also is possible that the teens saw the ubiquitous and typically risk-free sexual media content as encouragement for them to engage in sexual behavior sooner than they might have otherwise. It is most likely that both causal sequences are operating, but longitudinal studies of young adolescents are needed to conclude that with more certainty.

Cognitive Social Learning Theory and its earlier variant, Social Learning Theory, predict that people will imitate behaviors of others when those models are rewarded or not punished for their behavior. Modeling will occur more readily when the model is perceived as attractive and similar and the modeled behavior is possible, salient, simple, prevalent, and has functional value. Thus, the theory predicts that people who attend to media content that includes depictions of attractive characters who enjoy having sexual intercourse and rarely suffer any negative consequences will be likely to imitate the behavior.

A related idea is that the media provide cognitive scripts for sexual behavior that people may not be able to see anywhere else. Sexually inexperienced people especially may use the media to fill in the gaps in their understanding about how a particular sexual scenario might work (e.g., kissing goodnight at the end of a date, having sex with a new or multiple partners). . . .

What's typically missing from the media's current sexual script, however, is anything having to do with the possible negative consequences of sexual activity or ways to prevent negative outcomes, so it is unlikely that protective behavior could be imitated. Content analyses suggest that media audiences are most likely to learn that sex is consequence-free, rarely planned, and more a matter of lust than love. From the most sexually explicit media content, now more readily available than ever before on the Internet, cable TV, and videocassettes, they are likely to learn patterns of aggressive sexual behavior, as well.

In sum, the relatively few existing studies of the selection, interpretation, and application of sexual content in the media suggest that the mass media can affect awareness of, beliefs about, and possibly actual sexual behavior. More research is needed to say more precisely with which audiences, under what circumstances, and with which content effects occur. Such research is especially relevant as access to increasingly explicit sexual material increases and other potential perspectives on sexually responsible behavior, such as parents, schools, and faith communities, remain relatively reticent.

> "*I believe . . . strongly that there is a correlation between the explosion in sexual activity and the epidemics of STDs and depression in our teenagers.*"

Depression Shapes Teen Attitudes About Sex

Meg Meeker

In the following viewpoint Meg Meeker claims that there is a relationship between the rising rate of teen depression and teen sexual activity. She argues that teens who are depressed often turn to sex for comfort, and teens who are sexually active frequently become depressed. One reason for teen depression is parental divorce, in Meeker's view, which often pushes teens into sex at an early age. Meg Meeker is a pediatrician, author, and lecturer on teen issues.

As you read, consider the following questions:

1. What, according to Meeker, is the third leading cause of death among teenagers?
2. In the author's view, what is a classic example of youths turning their anger inward?
3. Why do teens repress their emotions following a divorce, in the author's opinion?

As a doctor, I can probe, culture, prescribe antibiotics, and aggressively treat and track contagious STDs [sexually transmitted diseases]. But depression is different. It's more elusive, yet equally, if not more, dangerous. It can come and go, or it can settle in, making itself so comfortable in an adolescent's psyche that it's nearly impossible to extricate. There, just as many STDs do, depression causes permanent damage that may not become apparent for years. To many teenagers, depression can make them feel as though another entity has moved into their body, taking over everything they think, feel, and do.

For the thousands of teens I've treated and counseled, one of the major causes of depression is sex. I consider it an STD with effects as devastating as—if not more—HPV, chlamydia or any other.

Just ask any doctor, therapist, or teacher who works closely with teenagers and they'll tell you: Teenage sexual activity routinely leads to emotional turmoil and psychological distress. Beginning in the 1970s, when the sexual revolution unleashed previously unheard-of sexual freedoms on college campuses across the country, physicians began seeing the results of this "freedom." This new permissiveness, they said, often led to empty relationships, to feelings of self-contempt and worthlessness. All, of course, precursors to depression.

Teens are particularly vulnerable to the negative effects of early sexual experience because of the intense and confusing array of emotions they're already experiencing. Adding sex to the picture only makes those feelings more intense and more confusing.

Like most STDs, depression remains hidden and under-diagnosed, even though its prevalence among our teenagers has skyrocketed in the past 25 years, paralleling the rise in STDs. We don't know exact numbers because so many of its victims can't put a name to their feelings, while too many adults pass off depressed behavior in teenagers as part of "normal adolescence." Other teenagers are so depressed they lack the energy or desire to seek help. For while physical pain drives patients to physicians, emotional pain keeps them away.

Still, the numbers we do have on depression in teens are

terrifying. According to Dr. John Graydon, professor of Psychiatry and Neurosciences at the University of Michigan, one in eight teenagers is clinically depressed and most teens' depression goes undetected. Because the rates of completed suicides among adolescents have skyrocketed 200% in the past decade, suicide now ranks as the third leading cause of death in teenagers, behind accidents and homicides (both of which may involve depressed adolescents, who often drink and engage in violent behavior to anesthetize their depressed feelings).

Also frightening is the fact that teens today are more likely to succeed in killing themselves when they try. One study found that completed suicides among 10- to 14-year-olds increased 80% from 1976 to 1980 and 100% for 15- to 19-year-olds. From 1980 to 1997, the rate of suicide increased 11% in all 15- to 19-year-olds, 105% in African-American teen boys, and a startling 109% in 10- to 14-year-old children. Even more sobering is the fact that for every adolescent who succeeds in committing suicide, 50 to 100 attempt it. In fact, a 1995 study found that a staggering 33 out of every 100 high school and middle school students said they'd thought of killing themselves.

One-third of our adolescent population has thought of killing themselves!

This statistic terrifies me, as it does countless parents, teachers, and grandparents in the country. Indeed, many experts on adolescent suicide and psychiatric illness refer to this dramatic increase as "a national tragedy." And I strongly believe, as do many of my colleagues, that the situation is much worse, that depression is highly underdiagnosed in teens. The bottom line is that depression has invaded millions of our teens. And that's just what we see on the surface.

I believe even more strongly that there is a correlation between the explosion in sexual activity and the epidemics of STDs and depression in our teenagers. I know this because of what I've heard from the thousands of teens I've counseled over the past 20 years, and from my own experiences raising four children. What I hear and see is that sexual freedom causes most of them tremendous pain. Now, research is just beginning to show a correlation between teen sex and STDs.

One study shows such a strong link between STDs and depression that the authors advised all physicians to screen every teen with an STD for depression. I go one step further—I screen all sexually active teens for depression, STD or not.

We already know that adults with STDs struggle with depression, guilt, and feelings of isolation and shame. And we know from several significant research studies that the breakup of teenage romantic relationships often leads to depression and alcohol abuse. One study of 8200 adolescents, ages 12 to 17, found that those involved in romantic relationships had significantly higher levels of depression than those not involved in romantic relationships. "Something about dating and dating relationships can be toxic to girls' health," says Susan Nolen-Hoeksema, Ph.D., a psychology professor at the University of Michigan in Ann Arbor, and an expert in adolescent depression. . . .

Sex and depression present a kind of chicken-and-egg conundrum. Studies find that kids who are depressed gravitate toward sex, since sex acts as a drug, numbing a hurt, filling a void, keeping their minds altered, if only for a moment. But sexual activity also leads to depression.

It's important here to understand the psychological roots of depression. In teens, depression is a prolonged state of grieving. Normally, one goes through a series of stages in resolving grief: denial, bitterness, anger, sadness, and acceptance. But if, for some reason, you experience hurt or loss and you *don't* go through this grieving process, depression can result.

For instance, a teenage boy may feel terrible sadness because he just broke up with his girlfriend, but he doesn't allow himself to exhibit that sadness for fear that someone (mom or dad perhaps) will notice and make fun of him. Or an adolescent girl who had sex and now feels guilty and confused may not allow herself to acknowledge these emotions, pushing them deep inside where they fester into depression.

This refusal to grieve takes the form of an unpeeled onion. The outer layer is denial that there is any problem, loss, or hurt. This is the most visible layer, and is obvious when teenagers insist I've got them figured all wrong, that they aren't depressed.

Beneath this layer of denial lies bitterness and anger. This anger stems from a sense of loss, and . . . there are numerous losses associated with sex. For instance, there is the loss of self-respect. Even if a teenager is mature enough to recognize this loss, if he doesn't move past the stage of anger to sadness, where he can grieve this loss, he may become "stuck" in anger at himself.

Sex and Teen Emotional Health

[According to a nationwide survey, there are] substantial differences in emotional health between those teens who are sexually active and those who are not:

> A full quarter (25.3 percent) of teenage girls who are sexually active report that they are depressed all, most, or a lot of the time. By contrast, only 7.7 percent of teenage girls who are not sexually active report that they are depressed all, most, or a lot of the time. Thus, sexually active girls are more than three times more likely to be depressed than are girls who are not sexually active.

> Some 8.3 percent of teenage boys who are sexually active report that they are depressed all, most, or a lot of the time. By contrast, only 3.4 percent of teenage boys who are not sexually active are depressed all, most, or a lot of the time. Thus, boys who are sexually active are more than twice as likely to be depressed as are those who are not sexually active.

Robert E. Rector, Kirk A. Johnson, and Lauren R. Noyes, "Sexually Active Teenagers Are More Likely to Be Depressed and to Attempt Suicide." Heritage Foundation, June 3, 2003. www.heritage.org.

Or a teenage girl may experience loneliness and a feeling of betrayal after a sexual relationship. If she fails to grieve those feelings properly, she may turn her hurt and anger inward, becoming "stuck" in persistent, unresolved anger and exhibiting harmful behavior, lashing out, stealing, engaging in self-destructive behavior (sex, drugs, alcohol). It may look like rage, but it is also depression.

One classic example of how kids turn this rage inward is the preponderance of body piercing. Punching holes in intimate parts of their bodies, such as their lips, tongue, belly button, or even vagina, sends a message to the world: "I am hurting this intimate part of myself because I don't like who I am." When girls pierce the sexual parts of their bodies, their labia and nipples (some so severely they'll never be able to nurse a baby), they're saying: "I am cutting on my womanhood. This is anger turned upon the self."

Beneath this anger often lies sadness. It's much safer and easier to feel the anger, I tell teens, than it is to feel this sadness. Anger lets energy out, whereas sadness only consumes energy. When you're sad, you want to be comforted, and too many teens have no one to comfort them. So they keep their sadness to themselves. The hurt stays like a crusted-over abscess on their hearts. Then they become angry with themselves because they're sad (irrational, yes, but this is teenager thinking), and angry with their family and friends because no one will help them get rid of their sadness or their anger.

At the center of this onion of depression is a hole—the empty space left when that which was so precious and prized is taken away. . . . Much is lost when teenagers have sex before they're ready. These losses are substantial, and can be devastating to the teenage soul. . . .

One of the greatest losses our teenagers feel is the loss inherent in divorce. When parents divorce, children experience both the physical loss of a parent and the concurrent feelings of abandonment and lack of control. Some teens can handle the death of a parent better than they do a divorce. At least, they rationalize, there is no choice in death.

As I've seen in my practice time and time again, divorce loss often propels kids into early sex. Let me explain.

We've seen this situation feebly played out on television countless times: Teens feel a large, undue responsibility for the divorce of their parents. It matters not how many times their parents reassure the teen that he or she is not responsible for the divorce. It's part of how a teen's mind works. A teenager's own adolescent self-centeredness and sense of power will negate rational thought, leaving him with pure emotion. As these losses accumulate, some require serious grieving.

Teens who have a good support system and a strong sense of connection with their parents or other adults are able to grieve losses to resolution. They allow themselves to feel their sadness, anger, and hurt, and even talk about them to friends and adults if they believe that their feelings will be respected.

Healthy parents are crucial to this process. We are the ones who provide the safe environment in which teens can feel and resolve their emotions. We need to be on the look-out for losses that occur in our children's lives so we can help them work through loss and resolve their hurt feelings.

But too often, teens suppress their emotions because they are simply too afraid to let them show at home. As children in our society grow into adolescence, they experience the loss of a sense of being protected, loved, and cared for.

Let's face it, too many teens are ignored in our culture. Within their own community, it seems everyone is too busy for them. Sometimes their doctor barely has time to talk to them; often both parents work and are too tired to talk when they come home; teachers are stretched thin by overcrowded classes; and psychiatrists have three-month waiting lists. I believe this generation of teens is the loneliest generation in the history of our country. Some parents push them away with the excuse that their kids need to become independent and world-savvy, when, in fact, parents just want their own lives. Kids require energy and patience, which many parents are often too tired to provide.

Too often, kids have no one with whom to figure out life, no one with whom to communicate their anger, sadness, or even the emptiness that life can bring. For teens to acknowledge that they never felt genuinely loved, never experienced healthy intimacy with a parent, and that no one of significance in their life really values them, would cause their world to cave in. Thus, they stuff it. They get stuck in depression. The onion stays unpeeled, an abscess at the center of their soul, waiting quietly for someone to prick it open and drain it.

That's when teens turn to sex, an action that relieves the momentary isolation, but which often leads to more loss in an endless cycle of emotional angst.

When I counsel teens who are depressed, I try to help them view themselves as whole people who have three dimensions—physical, psychological, and spiritual. I often explain that depression may start in one dimension and then spread to another.

The physical roots of depression generally stem from low levels of various neurochemicals, such as dopamine, norepinephrine, and serotonin. These chemicals play critical roles in the areas of energy, emotions, sensations, and cognition. Nerve endings in the brain release these chemicals, also called neurotransmitters, and they circulate throughout brain tissue until other nerve endings take them back up, similar to the way you suck up soda through a straw. If they aren't released in sufficient amounts, or are taken up too quickly before the brain has a chance to use them, depression can result.

I try to explain to teens that these physiological changes are completely real and completely out of their control. Just as someone with diabetes suffers from low levels of insulin, those with depression have altered levels of neurochemicals. No one asks for diabetes, no one asks for depression. Sometimes it just happens.

Serious depression can be caused by these imbalances, and for these types of illnesses, drug therapy is often the answer. But for the majority of physically healthy teens, this is not the cause. And unless I see clear signs of acute, long-term depression, we don't go the drug route.

The second dimension I talk about is the psychological, which I described earlier as "peeling back the onion." It's the layers of our subconscious, and as they emerge, these layers define who we are. In the case of depression, our psychological well-being depends greatly on how we handle denial, bitterness, anger, and other emotions as we move toward acceptance of difficult losses.

"Adolescents who are more religious hold more conservative views regarding sex."

Religion Influences Teen Sexual Attitudes

National Campaign to Prevent Teen Pregnancy

The National Campaign to Prevent Teen Pregnancy (NCPTP) in a nonprofit advocacy group. The NCPTP discusses the influence that religion has on teen sexual decisions in the following viewpoint. The organization argues that religion helps teens develop moral values and teaches them abstinence. The NCPTP concludes that strong religious faith in teens delays sexual activity and makes teens less likely to have permissive attitudes toward sex.

As you read, consider the following questions:

1. In the view of the NCPTP, how much representation has religion been given in the effort to reduce teen pregnancy?
2. Are religious teens less or more likely to use contraceptives, according to the authors?
3. Teen girls are especially likely to delay first sex when they are affiliated with which two religions, reports the NCPTP?

Barbara Dafoe Whitehead, Brian L. Wilcox, and Sharon Scales Rostosky, *Keeping the Faith: The Role of Religion and Faith Communities in Preventing Teen Pregnancy*. Washington, DC: National Campaign to Prevent Teen Pregnancy, 2001. Copyright © 2001 by the National Campaign to Prevent Teen Pregnancy. All rights reserved. Reproduced by permission.

Preventing teen pregnancy is as much about moral and re- ligious values as it is about public health. Teens, like adults, make decisions about their sexual behavior based in part on their values about what is right and wrong, what is proper and what is not. This is because sex is connected to as- pects of our lives that we hold most dear: our understanding of family and children, the meaning of love, marriage, and commitment, the role of self-expression and self-fulfillment, and, for many people, our relationships with God. While common sense tells us that faith leaders and faith communi- ties make a real difference in helping teens grow up healthy both physically and spiritually, a number of barriers have pre- vented the faith and secular sectors from working well to- gether to meet their common goal of helping teens avoid too-early pregnancy and parenting.

This . . . report, *Keeping the Faith: The Role of Religion and Faith Communities in Preventing Teen Pregnancy*, addresses what's behind some of those barriers, examines what research says about the role religion plays in teens' decisions about sex, and makes the argument for increased cooperation and understanding among secular and faith communities. . . . So- cial critic Barbara Dafoe Whitehead offers a reflection on overcoming the bridgeable divide between "faith talk" and "public health talk." Brian Wilcox, Sharon Scales Rostosky, and colleagues, [then provide] a comprehensive research re- view of the role of religiosity in teen sexual behavior. . . .

This report builds on five years of work by the National Campaign's Task Force on Religion and Public Values (RPV) to reach out to faith communities and to encourage community-based coalitions focused on preventing teen pregnancy to work with local religious leaders and institu- tions. In the first two years of the National Campaign, the members of the RPV Task Force, representing various faith traditions and secular perspectives, collaborated on a paper, "Religion, Public Values, and the Debate Over Teen Preg- nancy" (published in *While the Adults Are Arguing, the Teens Are Getting Pregnant: Overcoming Conflict in Teen Pregnancy Prevention*), which considered the range of religious and moral teachings on teen sexuality and related issues and the conflicts that often arise among these traditions. They concluded that faith communities, whatever their particular stances on the issue, are uniquely positioned to offer teens and their families moral instruction, faith-based activities, and a sense of community that would help reduce teen pregnancy rates. . . .

The Health/Faith Divide

Barbara Dafoe Whitehead, Ph.D., a member of the National Campaign's Task Force on Religion and Public Values, addresses a compelling question: why is it the case that so many efforts to reduce teen pregnancy have given only token representation—if any at all—to the perspectives of religion and faith? It's a particularly perplexing situation when one considers that most teens—like most adults—describe themselves as religious or spiritual. In fact, the most prevalent reason that virgin teen girls give for not engaging in sex is that it is against their religion or morals.

Whitehead begins with a description of what some have called "the health/faith divide" and investigates some of its historical origins. She ascribes much of the divide to the fundamental differences in the languages of faith and public health on sexuality—that is, the contrast between "God talk" and "health talk." Even when the two sectors agree on the same goal—say, abstinence for unmarried teens—they draw on very different traditions and values to describe why teens should adopt that behavior. But the religious sector is hardly homogeneous either; Whitehead also discusses the great diversity in opinion among faith communities on issues of teen sexuality.

Whitehead notes that faith leaders and communities play an important role in preventing teen pregnancy in at least three ways:

- They help young people develop morally and spiritually by transmitting the teachings and observances of their faith.
- They engage in activities that guide and protect young people and give them hope for the future—including offering education, youth groups, summer camps, youth sports leagues, tutoring programs, rites-of-passage observances, mentoring, and after school programs. These

youth development activities give teens productive things to do, offer them opportunities to gain knowledge, skills, and confidence, and, perhaps most importantly, connect them to caring adults.

- Some faith organizations explicitly address the issue of teen sexuality within the context of faith through sex and abstinence education, parent/child communication workshops, crisis pregnancy counseling, and referrals to family planning services.

Whitehead contends that faith communities have additional strengths to offer in the battle against teen pregnancy, including supporting hard-to-reach new immigrant parents and their children, as well as high-risk teens, especially young males, and building community-based coalitions across faiths and between faith groups and secular youth-serving organizations.

Strong Religious Views Decrease Teen Sex

Teens—particularly girls—with strong religious views are less likely to have sex than are less religious teens, largely because their religious views lead them to view the consequences of having sex negatively. According to a recent analysis of the [National Institute of Child Health and Human Development]-funded Add Health Survey, religion reduces the likelihood of adolescents engaging in early sex by shaping their attitudes and beliefs about sexual activity. . . .

"A better understanding of why religious adolescents are less likely to engage in early sexual intercourse may help in designing prevention programs for this behavior," said Duane Alexander, M.D., Director of the NICHD.

National Institute of Child Health and Human Development, "Strong Religious Views Decrease Teens' Likelihood of Having Sex," March 2003. www.nichd.nih.gov.

Finally, Whitehead offers hope that the divide between faith and public health is bridgeable. She suggests that adults look to teens themselves, who do not usually draw clear distinctions between the requirements of the body and the soul, for inspiration for how to bring the insights, perspectives, and efforts of faith communities to the broad-based campaign to reduce teen pregnancy in America.

The Role of Religiosity in Teen Sexual Behavior

But what does research tell us about the roles religious faith and practice play in the sexual behavior of teens? . . . Brian Wilcox, Ph.D., Sharon Scales Rostosky, Ph.D., and their colleagues examine 50 studies. They find support for the idea that religiosity (variously defined) is associated with delayed sexual activity among some groups of teens, while at the same time suggesting that some religious teens may be less likely to use contraception when they do begin sexual activity. However, the state of the research in this area is generally poor, which limits the conclusions one can draw. Here are some of the highlights from the review:

- *American teens are religious.* Roughly 90 percent of teens report being affiliated with a particular religious denomination, although fewer say they regularly participate in religious services or youth groups.
- *Religion and age.* Teens are less likely to participate in formal religious activities as they get older, although older teens are as likely as younger teens to say that religion is important to them.
- *Religion and gender.* Girls are more likely than boys to participate in worship services and religious activities and to rank religion as important to them.
- *Religion and race.* Black teens are much more likely than white teens to attach great importance to religion and usually have higher rates of weekly religious observance.
- *The role of religious attendance.* Regardless of gender or race, teens who attend services frequently are less likely to have permissive *attitudes* about sexual intercourse. More frequent attendance is associated with later sexual initiation for white males and for females generally. It also appears that frequent attendance is associated with increased contraceptive use among boys but decreased contraceptive use among girls.
- *The role of religious attitudes.* Adolescents who are more religious hold more conservative views regarding sex. However, attitudes and expectations typically are only moderately predictive of future behavior.
- *The effects of denominational affiliation.* Girls who are af-

filiated with either Catholic or fundamentalist Protestant denominations are especially likely to delay sexual debut, although they are less likely to use contraception once they do initiate sex. Girls with no religious affiliation tend to be younger when they first have sex. Some evidence suggests that boys with no religious affiliation have higher rates of sexual activity and lower rates of condom use.

Unfortunately, the surprisingly weak state of research in this field—particularly its lack of a strong theoretical base, use of narrow measures of religiosity, and lack of longitudinal studies, as well as the challenge of applying experimental designs to religion and faith—makes it difficult to disentangle the effect of religiosity on sexual behavior from the effect of sexual behavior on religious faith and practice or the effect of other factors affecting both religiosity and sexual behavior. What is clear, however, is that there is value in further exploring the connections between religion and teen sexual behavior, because the potential for faith and religion to reduce risky sexual behavior seems so promising.

More Research Is Necessary

In some ways, this report raises as many questions as it answers. Wilcox and his colleagues find that religious affiliation, faith, and practice appear to be related to teen sexual behavior, but the research is not yet strong enough to tell us exactly how and under what circumstances. And if religiosity can protect teens from risky sexual behavior, as the research suggests, what does that mean for faith communities? For religious leaders? For secular policymakers?

It is undoubtedly true that exciting and innovative programs exist in faith communities around the country, but we know almost nothing about the effectiveness of these interventions. Learning more about how these efforts work would be a benefit to both faith communities and to the broader society, particularly with the current interest in public funding of faith-based solutions to social problems. Of course, . . . religious leaders—like all leaders—do not make decisions based solely on research. In fact, some of the outcomes that faith communities may be most interested in—grace, forgiveness, salvation—are not amenable to empirical research.

In the final analysis, if moral values are at the center of the issue of teen pregnancy, then who better to involve in crafting solutions than faith leaders and faith communities? Issues of public funding aside, there is much that community coalitions to prevent teen pregnancy can do to help support the work of religious leaders and to harness the strengths of local institutions of faith. Similarly, given the disconnect between research on the role of religiosity on teen sexual behavior and polls that show that teens rank faith leaders low as important influences on their sexual decisionmaking, faith communities should feel challenged to do as much as they can to help teens make better decisions about sex.

|*"One important venue where adolescents can deal with their growing sexuality is the Internet."*

The Internet Influences Teen Sexual Attitudes

Kaveri Subrahmanyam, Patricia M. Greenfield, and Brendesha Tynes

Kaveri Subrahmanyam, Patricia M. Greenfield, and Brendesha Tynes are researchers with the Children's Digital Media Center at the University of California at Los Angeles. In the following viewpoint the authors contend that teens use the Internet to help construct their sexuality and identity. Subrahmanyam, Greenfield, and Tynes use conversations monitored in an online teen chat room as a basis for their analysis. The authors claim that the virtual world seems to offer a safe environment for teens to explore their sexuality and learn about sex.

As you read, consider the following questions:

1. According to the authors, how many 12–17-year-olds use the Internet?
2. What is the top source of information about sex for teens, in the view of Subrahmanyam, Greenfield, and Tynes?
3. In the opinion of the authors, what is the most common question directed at new entrants in a teen chat room?

Kaveri Subrahmanyam, Patricia M. Greenfield, and Brendesha Tynes, "Constructing Sexuality and Identity in an Online Teen Chat Room," *Journal of Applied Developmental Psychology*, vol. 25, November/December 2004, pp. 651–66. Copyright © 2004 by Elsevier, Inc. Reproduced by permission.

As the Internet has brought social interaction into the electronic domain, connecting electronic media with developmental processes has taken on increasing relevance. In this article, we explore the idea that adolescents' online interactions are both a literal and a metaphoric screen for representing two major adolescent developmental issues: sexuality and identity.

According to the survey conducted by the Pew Internet and American Life Project in Fall 2000, at least 17 million or 73% of all youth between 12 and 17 years use the Internet. Although they use the Internet for both instrumental purposes (e.g., for school work and finding educational material) and for social-communication purposes (e.g., communicating with friends, meeting new people, and joining groups), the communication uses of the Internet are much more popular among adolescents. These uses include applications such as instant messages, e-mail, chat rooms, bulletin boards, and Web logs or Blogs.

Although instant messages are the most popular communication modality among adolescents, their private nature makes them impossible to study in detail. In contrast, the public nature of Internet communication applications such as chat rooms, blogs, and bulletin boards affords us an open window into adolescent concerns, and so we examine the content of an online teen chat room in this article.

Of particular interest to us is the culture of online environments, such as chat rooms. We use the term culture to refer to that which is socially constructed and shared in interactive environments. Here, we are referring to the symbolic, not the material aspects of culture, including the linguistic codes, interactions, and discourse patterns found within online spaces. . . . In this article, we are concerned with how these symbolic devices are used to enact important adolescent concerns online, specifically the social construction of sexuality and identity. Our assumptions are that the culture of chat is an evolving one and is being constructed and shaped by the users themselves. Our study adopts a practice perspective, focusing on a particular type of media use that is woven into the fabric of everyday activity. In a chat room, participants are not simply interacting with media; they are also interacting with each other. . . .

According to the Kaiser Family Foundation survey conducted in Fall 2001, among online youth between 15 and 17 years, 71% were participating in chat rooms. Another estimate from the Pew study (2001) is that about 55% of online teens had visited a chat room. Whereas some chat rooms have a dedicated topic (for example, California teens, teens looking for romance, etc.), others have no dedicated topic (e.g., just hanging out, etc.). Our data come from one of the latter. An important feature of chat rooms is their anonymous nature. Although participants have first to register with a chat provider, most users probably provide only fictitious details about themselves. As part of the registration process, a user has to choose a screen name or nickname (also called a nick) that is visible when he/she is in a chat room. Users are advised to choose a name that does not reveal personal information (i.e., last name, phone number, etc.). Participants in a chat room are thus typically anonymous and disembodied to each other. Unless users divulge their real identity in the content of their conversation, participants in a chat room generally cannot "place" each other in the real world, either geographically or by name.

Teens Explore Sexuality in Chat Rooms

One major adolescent developmental issue is the construction of sexuality. During adolescence, sexual maturation is accompanied by increased sexual drive and interest in sex. Consequently, adolescents spend "time talking about sex, telling jokes, using sex slang, and exchanging sex-oriented literature." These activities are a way for adolescents to understand and control their sexual feelings. In fact, peer communication is the number-one source of information about sex for adolescents, followed by the media suggests that maintaining open communication with peers can serve as a coping mechanism for adolescents when dealing with the need for sexual expression.

One important venue where adolescents can deal with their growing sexuality is the Internet. As online chat rooms combine peer interaction with a popular medium, they may be especially suitable for adolescent sexual exploration, . . .

[but] youth who participate in chat rooms are also at greater risk for unwanted sexual solicitation. In fact [one study shows] that one sexual comment is made every 4 min in AOL teen chat rooms. This frequency should not be too surprising, given that peers and media are such important sources of sexual information for teens. However, little is known about what adolescents tell each other about sex in general and on the Internet in particular. The present study aims to fill this gap.

Arcadio. © by Cagle Cartoons, Inc. Reproduced by permission.

An increased sexual drive naturally prompts adolescents to initiate and engage in romantic relationships. That these relationships are a major source of concern to adolescents is illustrated by the finding that more than half of all the calls to a national telephone hotline dealt with relationship issues. Unfortunately, these new relationships are often accompanied by risky physical behaviors, such as engaging in unprotected sex. These physical dangers may be reduced when adolescents date and build romantic relationships online, even when they are engaging in cyber sex. (We define cyber sex as sexual arousal or masturbatory activity in response to interaction with an online partner.) In addition, Internet dating allows teenagers to maintain their anonymity and may lessen the emotional pain often associated with face-to-face dating. It may also allow girls to assume more authority in their interactions since obtaining and maintaining relationships is based on verbal skill, generally accepted as a female strong point. . . .

Another major developmental issue during adolescence is the construction of a psychosocial identity, which may be best viewed as a quest for self-understanding. The changes that occur during adolescence challenge the adolescent to find "his or her unique and consistent self-definition". According to [psychoanalysis expert Erik] Erikson, the psychosocial task facing adolescents is to develop sexual, moral, political, and religious identities that are relatively stable and consistent. Research suggests that adolescents make use of the media to learn about two important aspects of identity development—sex and gender. For instance, we know from previous work that adolescents use the multimedia environments of their rooms to express who they are and to learn about sexual and romantic scripts.

An important means for expressing gender, sexual, and other identities is the body. However, the online medium poses special problems as participants are disembodied from each other and so do not have information about one another's age, gender, race, or physical appearance (height, weight, etc.). Given the absence of "bodies" online and the fact that adolescence is a period when youth are experimenting with their identity, we were interested in examining identity expression in teen chat. . . .

Adolescents' peers and the partners they choose play an important role in the development of sexuality and identity. Indeed, an important feature of adolescence is the adolescent's need for close friends and desire for emotional fulfillment from friends. Young adolescents typically form small groups of friends, usually of the same sex and enjoy spending time and talking to each other. Often, they spend all day together at school and then come home and spend more time talking to each other, on the phone or in recent years, via instant messaging and chat. Subsequently, adolescence is characterized by heterosociality—which is the forming of "friendships with those of both sexes". Eventually, for heterosexual adolescents, group boy-girl relationships lead to paired relationships between members of the opposite sex. Adolescents commonly turn to these friends and romantic partners for intimacy and companionship. Past research has tended to see adolescent romance merely as a context for sexuality. However, chat now enables us to view adolescent romance in the context of adolescent peer culture and peer relationships, whose evanescent quality has made it somewhat inaccessible to research in the past. Furthermore, given that romantic relationships are a major topic of adolescent conversation, online chat can make this conversation potentially visible to researchers for the first time. . . .

A Wide Range of Sex Topics Are Discussed

The quantitative study of sexual comments in teen chat had indicated that sexuality was important in chat, and the presence of a "sex thread" replicates that finding here. Looking at this thread in more detail, we find a broad range of sexual topics that were the subject of peer discussion. Although the conversation began with the topic of abortion, it quickly digressed to related topics such as pre-marital sex and birth control devices such as condoms. The adolescent preoccupation with sex is evident in the following extract from the conversation:

548. Immaculate ros: sex sex sex that all you think about?

559. Snowbunny: people who have sex at 16 r sick :-(

560: Twonky: I agree

564. 00o0CaFfEiNe: no sex until ur happily married . . . thatz muh rule

566. Twonky: I agree with that too

567. Snowbunny: me too caffine!

In our 2000 transcript, we found a similar concern with sex, but, in that instance, with the sexually developing body; there participants discussed the merits and demerits of Speedo swimsuits as they show off sexual anatomy, especially of boys. In both examples, the special contribution of the online medium is that its anonymous nature allows participants to have a frank discussion of a potentially embarrassing topic. Note too that participants can get information by "lurking" or just hanging out in the chat room. . . .

Teens Find Internet Pornography Without Looking

American children live in an "all-pervasive sexualized media environment" that produces a "tremendous amount of inadvertent exposure to pornography and other adult sexual media." Teenagers are routinely exposed to values on the Internet that would disturb many parents; teens often search the Internet for information about sex that they would be embarrassed to discuss with an adult. . . .

Not only will children seeking pornography "find it all over the Internet," but children who are not seeking pornography are often inadvertently exposed to it when they conduct Internet searches on perfectly appropriate subjects, said Patricia Greenfield, UCLA psychology professor and director of UCLA's Children's Digital Media Center (CDMC).

"Childhood used to be a time of relative innocence for many children," Greenfield said, "but with today's all-pervasive sexualized media environment, that is no longer the case. By late childhood, it has become very difficult to avoid highly sexualized material that is intended for an adult audience."

Stuart Wolpert, "Teenagers Find Information About Sex on the Internet When They Look for It—And When They Don't, UCLA's Children's Digital Media Center Reports," *UCLA News*, March 14, 2005. http://newsroom.ucla.edu.

Capitalizing on the alphanumeric nature of the chat environment, participants utilize another cultural solution to give and get fundamental identity-related information about potential conversation partners. The solution is the ubiquitous a/s/l (age/sex/location) chat code. . . . According to the Pew Internet report (2001), titled "Teenage Life Online", online teens report that the a/s/l code is the most common question directed toward new entrants in a chat room.

The a/s/l code is particularly interesting to us because we know . . . that age and sex are the primary categories to which people are assigned. Clearly, both these pieces of information are immediately evident in face-to-face encounters. Within the ambiguous nature of the chat environment, however, they are not evident and have to be made explicit. Location, a third category of information, is so fundamental that it is taken for granted in face-to-face interactions; it most definitely cannot be taken for granted on the Internet and must be made explicit. [There are] two ways that the a/s/l code is used in a teen chatroom. One primary use of the a/s/l code is as a conversation opener—users frequently type a/s/l to find out the characteristics of others in the room. . . .

Teens Use Chat for Cyber Pickups

Our analysis suggests that one way by which participants identified a potential partner with whom to "pair off" was by combining disclosure of basic identity characteristics, with a request for numerals. Before going further, it may be useful to describe the "cyber pickup". It occurs when one person makes a sexualized advance to another with the goal of going off into a private, dyadic Instant Message space.

In line #276 below, TVHMJ provides basic identity information about herself and asks interested partners to identify themselves by pressing 12345. By identifying herself with the adjectives "hot" and "sexy", the speaker conveys that she is looking for sexual intimacy in a conversational partner. However, note that she does not specify which gender she wants her conversational partner to be. Here, TVHMJ does not receive a public response immediately and this may be why she repeats her utterance two more times (line #296 and 326). The lack of response (12345) in the transcript suggests a lack of interest in her particular identity. She had revealed herself to be 13 years old and might have been considered too young by the other participants. . . .

276. TVHMJ: who wants to chat with a hot and sexy 13/f/ct press 12345

296. TVHMJ: who wants to chat with a hot and sexy 13/f/ct press 12345

326. TVHMJ: who wants to chat with a hot and sexy 13/f/ct press 12345

Our transcript from 2000 had indicated that a prerequisite for a successful cyber pickup might be divulging one's own information about age, sex, and location. However, this strategy does not work for TVHMJ, probably because the information was not attractive to the other chatters.

An example of successful partner selection is illustrated below. The beginning of the example shows FoxyR making numerous attempts to find a partner. Finally, in lines 262 and 264, she explicitly declares her identity as a "hot chick" and invites those who want to chat with her to "press 1234". At this DEREKH01 responds with "1234" in line 266. Although we cannot be sure, it appears that she asks interested parties to Instant Message her (line 268). FoxyR is not heard from again until line 304. This may be because she was having an instant message conversation with DEREKH01; however, because of the private nature of Instant messaging, we have no way of confirming this from the chat transcript.

210. FoxyR: wasssssssssup yallllllllllll

212. FoxyR: anybody here like 50 cent press 1234

214. FoxyR: 1234

221. FoxyR: wassssssssssup

222. FoxyR: wanna chat

262. FoxyR: any body wanna chat with a hot chick

263. Kdubon40: being the biggest jv player i dont get hit by bigger guys

264. FoxyR: press 1234

265. Breethebrat: if there r any m/13/Tx in here if so im me

266. DEREKH01: 1234

268. FoxyR: i amame

304. FoxyR: any body wa nna chat

It is interesting that these examples as well as the ones below were initiated by girls.

516. InsulentBrat1004: any single guys in here if so im me or press 252

582. Lilangal: hey any rally hott guys wanna chat to a really hott girl im me or press 23456

They point to the possibility that online chat is liberating for adolescent girls when it comes to initiating intimate relationships. . . . Since the advent of computer-mediated communication, researchers have suggested that the relative anonymity and absence of bodies on the Internet may liberate women from an often subordinate position. Notwithstanding our finding that participants use implicit ways to give and get information about gender, these examples suggest that adolescent girls may be able to initiate online relationships with the opposite sex without much of the weight of traditional gender roles and without the possible stigmatization for being too forward.

The Internet Provides Common Ground for Teens

In this article, we have shown how the online medium provides adolescents with a venue wherein they can and do deal with the same developmental issues as in their offline lives. In the case of sexuality, it provides a place to discuss embarrassing topics in an anonymous social context. It also provides a relatively safe place to "practice" new kinds of relationships, such as dating, that can be risky in the real world. Relative to offline dating, benefits are reduced; but so are the risks that come with face-to-face interaction. For example, rejection in an online setting with strangers probably stings less than one from a known other. On the other hand, the online chat environment has its own special dangers— such as unwanted cybersexual solicitation.

We also see that the categories of identity are just as salient online as off and that teens go to great lengths to overcome the "facelessness" and "placelessness" of the medium to present themselves and learn about the critical categories of identity of others. We found a high concordance between stated gender identity and the more implicit message conveyed by the nicknames. At the same time, a minority of participants used nicknames to express some other part of their identity rather than gender or sexuality. All in all, placement in the categories of age, sex, and location, plus expressions of gender identity in nicknames, provide a means for intimate pairing off with a peer. Consequently, the medium is not doing something to adolescents; they, instead, are doing something with the medium. Teen chat provides new affordances for old adolescent issues. . . .

In the highly mobile society of today, media provide common ground for all adolescents and are an important socialization agent for adolescents. According to [University of

Maryland researcher and author J.J.] Arnett, adolescents have considerable freedom and choice about the materials that they draw from the media—the materials that then contribute to their socialization. Thus, "when they use media materials towards identity formation or coping, when they participate in a media-based youth subculture, adolescents are also, in a larger sense, participating in activities that are part of their socialization." Importantly, as pointed out by Arnett, media as a socialization agent, are more similar to peers than other agents such as family, school, or community. Since adolescents choose both their media and their peer group, they have more control over their socialization from these agents compared to their socialization from agents over which they have less control, such as their family or school.

"Most (89%) primary care physicians felt comfortable discussing sexual-related issues with their patients."

Physicians Shape Teen Attitudes About Sex

Jeffrey K. Clark, Rebecca A. Brey, and Amy E. Banter

Jeffrey K. Clark and Rebecca A. Brey are associate professors in the department of physiology and health science at Ball State University, and Amy E. Banter, a physician, is associate director of the Family Practice Center at Ball Memorial Hospital, Muncie, Indiana. In the following viewpoint Clark, Brey, and Banter discuss the impact physicians have on teen sexual attitudes. The authors state that doctors can play an important role in reducing risky sexual behavior among teens and directing them to resources that promote healthy sexual behavior.

As you read, consider the following questions:

1. Do teens and parents want doctors to take an active role in education on sexual behavior, according to the authors?
2. Are moral messages by doctors about sexual behavior effective with teens, in the opinion of Clark, Brey, and Banter?
3. The authors state that schools often have programs where doctors provide what type of service to teens?

Jeffrey K. Clark, Rebecca A. Brey, and Amy E. Banter, "Physicians as Educators in Adolescent Sexuality Education," *Journal of School Health*, vol. 73, December 2003, pp. 389–91. Copyright © 2003 by the American School Health Association. Reproduced by permission.

The Centers for Disease Control and Prevention (CDC) identified risky sexual behavior as one of six health behaviors most associated with mortality, morbidity, and social problems among youth. In 2001, nearly 46% of youth in the United States had engaged in sexual intercourse, while more than 14% had four or more lifetime sex partners. Approximately 58% used a condom during their last intercourse, and 18% reported using birth control pills before their last intercourse.

Patterns of risky sexual behavior, often established before adulthood, may correlate with other risk behaviors, such as delinquency and drug use, to form a "risk behavior syndrome." The risk behavior syndrome suggests multiple risks should be addressed together in prevention programs.

The eight components of a coordinated school health program can support multiple programs designed to address the multiple risks of today's youth. For example, school health instruction can provide information and skills to make decisions about one's health. School health service programs can provide resources for youth to successfully change their health behavior while providing a unique opportunity for physicians to play an active role in adolescent health promotion.

Historically, support for sexuality education has been strong. Parental support for sexuality education carries over to include support for school health service programs. Education goals for the year 2000, as well as other education initiatives, voiced support for coordination and collaboration of health, education, and social services with school organizations. The School Health Policies and Programs Study (SHPPS) documented that 97% of all public schools offer some level of health services, and more than 40% offered STD [sexually transmitted diseases], pregnancy prevention, and prenatal referrals. In some schools, school-based health centers provide the only source of regular care for students without medical coverage.

Many organizations play an important role in helping adolescents develop a healthy sexuality. Adolescents receive information from a variety of sources, including family, peers, school, faith-based organizations, media, and medical personnel. The role of the physician as a sexuality educator often goes overlooked, though parents and adolescents are united in wanting physicians to take a proactive role in educating adolescents about sexual risk behavior.

Physicians Are Part of Health Team

Physicians represent an important member of the school health team. In addition to meeting the health needs of students, faculty, and staff, they reinforce and provide credibility to health promotion messages. The combination of one-on-one interaction, and the confidentiality of the physician/patient relationship, can encourage frank and honest discussions.

Physicians play an important role in reducing adolescents' sexual risks. The Guidelines for Adolescent Preventive Services (GAPS) recommend that "all adolescent . . . patients should be advised about risk factors for human immunodeficiency virus (HIV) and other sexually transmitted diseases, and counseled . . . to reduce risk of infection." While few studies measured the effectiveness of physicians at influencing high-risk sexual behavior of adolescents, consistent evidence shows that American adults changed their behavior in response to information about HIV and other STDs through public education and medical encounters. Patient education about lifestyle issues has proved helpful in changing risky behavior. In addition, the one-on-one interaction of patient education allows for messages tailored to the needs of individuals that can be effective in facilitating behavior change. For example, physician counseling related to smoking can increase patient participation in smoking cessation, and HIV counseling has resulted in reduction of risky behaviors. The time needed to incorporate such positive messages has been estimated at as little as four to seven minutes.

Parents and adolescents consider physicians and school-based clinics as credible sources of sexuality information. [George Washington University Medical Center researcher Bradley O.] Boekeloo and colleagues found that "adolescents typically said their physician's opinion would be about as important as or more important than their mother's, father's, or best friend's opinions" if they were considering having sex. In another study, healthcare providers were named more frequently than parents and peers as a source of information about sexual intercourse, birth control, STDs, pregnancy, and unwanted sexual activity. Adolescents also reported that they found it easy to talk with their physician during their visit. However, nearly one-half of the adolescents indicated that they would never ask an embarrassing question of their physician.

[Sexuality researcher and author] S.B. Jensen and L.R. Schover showed that only 10% of patients with sexual concerns were assertive enough to request help. Because patients are not likely to initiate discussions concerning sexual matters, physicians who do not introduce the topic miss a valuable opportunity to influence an adolescent's life. Physicians should take a more active role in creating an atmosphere where their adolescent patients feel comfortable discussing sexual matters.

Most (89%) primary care physicians felt comfortable discussing sexual-related issues with their patients, but less than one-third believed they were effective at changing risky sexual behavior. Nationally, 56% of physicians "usually or always" ask their patients about STDs, far below the nearly 90% of primary care physicians who felt comfortable discussing sexual issues with their patients. Even fewer physicians take a sexual history sufficiently detailed to counsel patients about HIV risk behaviors.

Developing Rapport with Teens

Physicians should establish a comfortable relationship with adolescents regardless of the practice setting. Educational and social interaction at schools, establishing and working with school clinics, and speaker events provide some traditional ways physicians can develop rapport with adolescents. Yet, time constraints and lack of reimbursement for services often create barriers to these approaches. Thus, physicians should begin exploring ways to increase the comfort level of their adolescent patients in the clinical setting.

Interacting with a same-gender physician may, in some cases, improve the perceived approachability of the physician. However, in most cases gender issues can be overcome.

Initial considerations for working with adolescents in a clinical setting begin with a positive attitude toward adolescent patients regardless of their gender. Using moral messages about behavior, or use of "you should" or "you must" statements, tends to be ineffective. Rapport cannot develop if patients know the physicians feel embarrassed, dislike teenagers, or feel uncomfortable with their own sexuality.

Teen Sexuality and the Primary Care Physician

The teenager's primary care physician is of paramount importance. It is the physician who provides a safe and secure environment where the adolescent can explore and discuss sexual issues. The physician should be open, honest, interested, concerned, and supportive and, in addition, be able to communicate in a manner appropriate to the teen's developmental stage.

Asking the teen "Do you date boys, girls, or both?" conveys the clinician's openness to issues regarding homosexuality. Even if the teenager is not yet ready to this discussion, the clinician has broached the topic; the disclosure can thus occur when the young person is ready.

Mary Desmond Pinkowish, "Adolescent Medicine: Teen Sexuality," *Patient Care*, January 2003. www.patientcareonline.com.

Understanding risk factors contributing to adolescent sexual behavior may provide openings for initiating interaction with adolescents. Religiosity, socioeconomic status, gender, family structures, communication with parents, and scholastic achievement represent important nonthreatening topics that physicians can use to initiate conversations about sexual behavior. Information regarding these topics can help physicians establish rapport, as well provide an assessment of the likelihood for sexual activity by the adolescent patient.

After recognizing the possibility of sexual activity and determining risk behaviors, physicians also should consider developmental issues. Using the GAPS implementation materials as a basis for the patient interview provides a good starting point for interaction with adolescent patients. The 11 items from the development section of the "Middle-Older Adolescent Questionnaire" may provide a means to initiate discussion of sexuality issues. Any item eliciting a positive response can lead to a patient education opportunity. Even when adolescents reply negatively to all the items, physicians may select a couple of items to initiate patient education on sexuality topics. Based on the information gathered, physicians decide the specific developmentally appropriate sexuality message for the patient.

Providing services that help prepare adolescents before their visit may be necessary. [Researchers] found that studying physician education materials (eg, video, risk assessment, and brochure) prior to a visit with their physicians created little impact on the number of sexuality topics physicians and their adolescent patients discussed. However, when adolescents received patient education tools, the number of sexuality topics discussed with their physicians increased.

The Power of the Physician

The goal of patient education for sexuality should focus on helping adolescents sort out their feelings, make decisions about behavior and risk reduction, understand the consequences of their behavior, and identify resources to assist in promoting positive health behavior. These skills can be incorporated with other preventive health messages. Health educators need to recognize the power of physician recommendation on individual adolescent behavior change, and encourage physicians' support for sexuality education through communication and providing opportunities for interaction with adolescents outside the physician's office.

The potential for partnership between physicians and health educators must be explored and developed more fully. Schools often have programs where physicians provide sport physicals and other services. Scheduling adequate time for physicians to provide comprehensive, personalized interaction may create an environment where sexuality issues can be addressed.

School health educators, especially teachers, interact with adolescents over a much longer time period than do physicians, and can introduce and reinforce prevention messages. Health educators can assist physicians by providing information or materials that incorporate prevention messages readily implemented by adolescents. Additional collaboration between health educators and physicians may lead to creation and extended use of developmentally appropriate materials that address sexuality issues in education and clinic settings. Consequently, communication between physicians and health educators working with the same adolescent population must be frequent and ongoing.

Though health educators and physicians provide different types and levels of preventive services related to sexuality issues, the goals are the same: to improve and maintain healthy sexuality among youth. Collaboration of health educators and physicians can make a difference and reduce risk behavior in adolescents.

Periodical Bibliography

The following articles have been selected to supplement the diverse views presented in this chapter.

R.L. Collins — "Watching Sex on Television Predicts Adolescent Initiation of Sexual Behavior," *Canadian Journal of Human Sexuality*, March 2004.

Margery Eagan — "Old Adult Taboo No Match for Teen Cynicism," *Boston Herald*, February 23, 2005.

Marilyn Elias — "TV May Push Teens to Start Sex Earlier," *Deseret News*, September 7, 2004.

Dina Gerdeman — "Teen Survey: In Matters of Sex, Friends Rule," *Patriot Ledger*, May 21, 2002.

John Gutierrez-Mier — "Youth Views About AIDS Worry Some," *Star-Telegram*, March 27, 2004.

Douglas Kirby — "The Impact of Schools and School Programs upon Adolescent Sexual Behavior," *Journal of Sex Research*, February 2002.

Susan J. Landers — "Doctors Can Bridge Sex Knowledge Gap for Teens," *AMedNews*, August 23, 2004.

Patricia Lefevere — "Sex and Sensibility: A Faith-Based View: Sex Educator Tackles Tough Issues with Young Teens," *National Catholic Reporter*, September 19, 2003.

Brent C. Miller — "Family Influences on Adolescent Sexual and Contraceptive Behavior," *Journal of Sex Research*, February 2002.

Mary Ellen Schneider — "Teen Sex and Suicide—Policy & Practice," *OB/GYN News*, July 15, 2003.

Alan A. Stone — "Loss of Innocence: Sex, Drugs, and Peer Group Pressure in Middle School," *Psychiatric Times*, January 2004.

David Vincent — "Revenge of the Nerds: Out Go Pecs and Testosterone, and in Come Specs and Sexual Ambiguity," *Mail on Sunday*, February 13, 2005.

Jeff Wright — "Teen Sex Challenges Churches," *Register-Guard*, October 17, 2004.

CHAPTER 2

Should Society Be Concerned About Teen Sex?

Chapter Preface

In asking the question, "Should society be concerned about teen sex?" conservatives and liberals answer quite differently. In general, conservatives believe that teen sex is wrong and should be discouraged while liberals view teen sex more positively, focusing on limiting the dangers associated with teen sexual activity rather than trying to stop it.

Many conservatives believe that sexual activity has negative physical and psychological consequences for young people. They argue that abstinence is the only sure way to prevent the unintended pregnancies and sexually transmitted diseases (STDs) associated with teen sex. In general, they support the teaching of abstinence until marriage and disapprove of comprehensive sex education that teaches young people to use condoms. According to many conservatives, studies show that students who participate in abstinence-only programs wait longer to have sex than students who do not and are therefore shielded from many of the dangers associated with sex.

In contrast, liberals claim that most people do not wait until marriage to have sex, so young people, who are quite likely to engage in some kind of sexual activity, should learn to protect themselves from unwanted pregnancies and diseases. Most liberals believe that comprehensive sex education results in teens being less likely to be sexually active and more likely to use condoms. They point out that rates of sexual activity among teens are comparable in Europe and the United States, but northern European teens have lower rates of pregnancy and STDs because they have more access to and knowledge of contraceptives.

Clearly, how a group views teen sex determines the kinds of programs it will support. The deep rift between conservatives and liberals concerning teenage sexual activity has resulted in endless battles over sex education, condom distribution, and abortion rights. The authors in this chapter, writing from both a conservative and liberal perspective, investigate how society should view teen sex. Given the chasm that separates these two groups, the debate is likely to continue well into the future.

| "*Teen pregnancy is closely linked to a host of other critical social issues—welfare dependency and overall child well-being, out-of-wedlock births, responsible fatherhood, and workforce development.*"

Teen Pregnancy Is a Serious Problem

National Campaign to Prevent Teen Pregnancy

The National Campaign to Prevent Teen Pregnancy (NCPTP) is a nonprofit youth advocacy group. In this viewpoint the organization argues that despite declining birth rates among U.S. girls, teen pregnancy is still a national problem. The organization claims that teen pregnancy is linked to a number of other social problems, including poverty and welfare dependency. The organization also argues that teen pregnancy has serious economic consequences.

As you read, consider the following questions:
1. What country, according to the author, has the highest rate of teen pregnancy among industrialized nations?
2. In the view of the NCPTP, continuing to reduce teen pregnancy will help decrease what two problems?
3. Children born to teen parents are often denied a close relationship with whom, according to the author?

Teen pregnancy is closely linked to a host of other critical social issues—welfare dependency and overall child well-being, out-of-wedlock births, responsible fatherhood, and workforce development in particular. The National Campaign to Prevent Teen Pregnancy believes that preventing teen pregnancy should be viewed not only as a reproductive health issue, but as one that works to improve all of these measures. Simply put, if more children in this country were born to parents who are ready and able to care for them, we would see a significant reduction in a host of social problems afflicting children in the United States, from school failure and crime to child abuse and neglect.

The facts compiled below provide compelling evidence that progress on all of these issues is materially advanced by reducing teen pregnancy. We urge policymakers, advocates, and others interested in one or more of these social policy issues to give serious attention to preventing teen pregnancy and to be encouraged by the growing variety of effective interventions as well as the strong public consensus that teen pregnancy is a serious problem which needs to be addressed. . . .

Teen Pregnancy Is Still a Major Problem

Less sexual activity among teens and increased contraceptive use have both contributed to the encouraging declines in the teen pregnancy and birth rates during the 1990s. Teen pregnancy rates are at their lowest level in 20 years and teen birth rates are at the lowest level ever recorded in this country. These trends show that progress can be made on what was once seen as an intractable social problem. However, we still have a long way to go:

- Despite the recent good news, the United States still has the *highest* rates of teen pregnancy, birth, and abortion in the fully industrialized world.
- Four in ten girls become pregnant at least once before age 20—over 900,000 teen pregnancies annually.
- There are nearly half a million teen births each year. Put another way, each hour nearly 100 teen girls get pregnant and 55 give birth.
- About 40 percent of pregnant teens are 17 or younger.

- Nearly eight in ten pregnancies among teens are not planned or intended.
- At present, 79 percent of births to teen mothers are out-of-wedlock—a dramatically different picture from 30 years ago when the vast majority of births to teen mothers were within marriage.
- Some teens are having sex earlier. One major data set indicates that the only group of teen girls showing an increase in sexual activity is those under age 15. And, a 1999 study indicated that 8.3 percent of students report having sex before age 13—a disturbing 15 percent increase since 1997.
- Many of the fathers of children born to teen mothers are older; almost half of young men who impregnate a minor teen (under 18) are three or more years older.
- The overall declines have masked high rates that exist for certain teens, defined by geography, age, and racial or ethnic group. For example, in some states, the teen pregnancy problem has gotten worse in selected communities.
- Among Hispanics, the fastest growing ethnic group in the nation, teen birth rates have declined more slowly than for other groups over the 1990s and Hispanics now have the highest teen birth rate nationally. Birth rates for Hispanic teens have actually increased in a number of states.
- Between 1995 and 2010, the number of girls aged 15–19 will increase by 2.2 million. If current fertility rates remain the same, we will see a 26 percent increase in the number of pregnancies and births among teenagers.

The 1990s have brought good news: Both teen pregnancy and birth rates have declined nationwide, in all states, and among all age and racial/ethnic groups. However, this progress in preventing teen pregnancy can have a downside if it means that the public, policymakers, and the media begin to believe that the teen pregnancy problem has been solved. The hard truth is that yesterday's good news about declining teen pregnancy and birth rates won't mean much to the boys and girls who turn 13 next year. We must guard against complacency, and we must redouble our efforts to convince each new group of young people that it is in their own self-interest and that of future generations to avoid early pregnancy and childbearing.

Teen Pregnancy Prevention Is a Good Investment

Not only does teen childbearing have serious consequences for teen parents, their children, and society; it also has important economic consequences. Helping young women avoid too-early pregnancy and childbearing—and young men avoid premature fatherhood—is easier and much more cost effective than dealing with all of the problems that occur after the babies are born.

- Teen childbearing costs taxpayers at least $7 billion each year in direct costs associated with health care, foster care, criminal justice, and public assistance, as well as lost tax revenues.
- A cost benefit analysis suggests that the government could spend up to eight times more than is currently being spent on teen pregnancy prevention and still break even.
- A study estimating the cost-effectiveness and cost-benefit of one particular curriculum found that for every dollar invested in the program, $2.65 in total medical and social costs were saved. The savings were produced by preventing pregnancy and sexually transmitted diseases (STDs).
- If teen birth rates had stayed at the level they were in the early 1990s, 125,468 more babies would have been born to teens.

Teen Pregnancy and Poverty

Continuing to reduce teen pregnancy will sustain the recent decreases in welfare dependency and poverty, especially persistent child poverty. Poverty is a cause as well as a consequence of early childbearing, and some impoverished young mothers may end up faring poorly no matter when their children are born. Nevertheless, most experts agree that although disadvantaged backgrounds account for many of the burdens that young women shoulder, having a baby during adolescence only makes matters worse:

- Compared to women of similar social-economic status who postpone childbearing, teen mothers are more likely to end up on welfare.
- Almost one-half of all teen mothers and over three-quarters of unmarried teen mothers began receiving welfare within five years of the birth of their first child.
- Some 52 percent of all mothers on welfare had their first child as a teenager.
- Teen mothers are less likely to complete the education necessary to qualify for a well-paying job—only 41 percent of mothers who have children before age 18 ever complete high school compared with 61 percent of similarly situated young women who delay childbearing until age 20 or 21.
- Virtually all of the increase in child poverty between 1980 and 1996 was related to the increase in nonmarital childbearing, and half of never-married mothers begin their childbearing as teens.

Births Per 1,000 Teens Aged 15–19 (1995–1998)

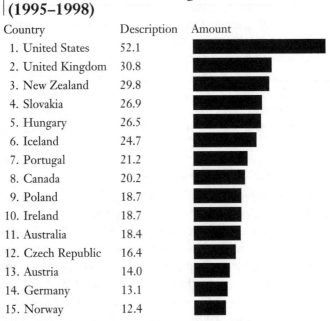

Country	Description	Amount
1. United States	52.1	
2. United Kingdom	30.8	
3. New Zealand	29.8	
4. Slovakia	26.9	
5. Hungary	26.5	
6. Iceland	24.7	
7. Portugal	21.2	
8. Canada	20.2	
9. Poland	18.7	
10. Ireland	18.7	
11. Australia	18.4	
12. Czech Republic	16.4	
13. Austria	14.0	
14. Germany	13.1	
15. Norway	12.4	

United Nations Children's Fund, 2001. www.nationmaster.com.

- Two-thirds of families begun by a young unmarried mother are poor.
- Nearly 80 percent of fathers of children born to teen mothers do not marry the mothers. These fathers pay less than $800 annually in child support, often because they are quite poor themselves. Since child support can be an important source of income for poor children, children born to young fathers are at further disadvantage.
- Teen mothers are likely to have a second birth relatively soon—about one-fourth of teenage mothers have a second child within 24 months of the first birth—which can further impede their ability to finish school or keep a job, and to escape poverty.

In addition to the goal of moving welfare recipients into work, the 1996 federal welfare reform law placed a strong emphasis on reducing out-of-wedlock childbearing and teen pregnancy. Welfare caseloads have declined dramatically since 1996 and millions of low-income parents have moved into the labor force. Child poverty rates have also declined significantly. However, this progress could be short-lived if every welfare recipient who goes to work and begins moving toward self-sufficiency is replaced by a pregnant younger sister, or daughter, who is not prepared to support a family. To sustain the progress made to date, it is important to implement policies and invest resources that help young people—both girls and boys—avoid premature pregnancy and childbearing.

Teen Pregnancy and Child Well-Being

Reducing teen pregnancy will enhance child well-being. The children of teen mothers bear the greatest burden of teen pregnancy and childbearing, and are at significantly increased risk for a number of economic, social, and health problems:

- The children of teen mothers are more likely to be born prematurely and at low birthweight, raising the probability of infant death, blindness, deafness, chronic respiratory problems, mental retardation, mental illness, cerebral palsy, dyslexia, and hyperactivity.
- Children of teen mothers do worse in school than those born to older parents. They are 50 percent more likely

to repeat a grade, are less likely to complete high school than the children of older mothers, and have lower performance on standardized tests.

- The children of teen parents also suffer higher rates of abuse and neglect than would occur if their mothers had delayed childbearing.
- The sons of teen mothers are 13 percent more likely to end up in prison.
- The daughters of teen parents are 22 percent more likely to become teen mothers themselves.

Smith. © 1996 by North American Syndicate. Reproduced by special permission.

A key conclusion that emerges from all these sobering facts is this: Preventing teen pregnancy is critical to improving not only the lives of young women and men but also the future prospects of their children. Indeed, one of the surest ways to improve overall child well-being is to reduce the proportion of children born to teen mothers.

Teen Pregnancy and Marriage

Reducing teen pregnancy will decrease out-of-wedlock childbearing and increase the percentage of children born to married couples. While the majority of non-marital births are to adult women, the teen years are frequently a time when unmarried families are first formed—a strong rationale for focusing on teens in any broad effort to reduce out-of-wedlock chiidbearing.

- Although only three out of ten out-of-wedlock births in the United States are to teenagers, nearly half (48 percent) of all non-marital *first* births occur to teens—the largest single group.
- Nearly 80 percent of teen births are to unmarried teens, up from 15 percent in 1960.
- Men and women today marry, on average, three to four years later than did their counterparts in the 1950s. As a result of later marriage and both earlier menarche and earlier age of first sex, teens today begin having sex roughly eight years before marriage.
- In contrast with the 1960s and 1970s, when most of the growth of single-parent families was caused by increases in divorce or separation, nearly all of the growth in the 1980s and 1990s has been driven by increases in out-of-wedlock childbearing.
- Teen mothers spend more of their young adult years as single parents than do women who delay childbearing.
- Only 30 percent of teen mothers who marry after their child is born remain in those marriages and teen marriages are twice as likely to fail as marriages in which the woman is at least 25 years old. . . .

Clearly, helping more women reach adulthood before they have children would go a long way toward ensuring that more children grow up in stable, married families. And considering the large body of research on the benefits to children of growing up in such families, the link between reducing teen pregnancies and improving overall child well-being is clear.

Teen Pregnancy and Responsible Fatherhood

Reducing teen pregnancy contributes significantly to the goal of promoting responsible fatherhood. Research shows that involved and committed fathers are important to the well-being of their children. But unfortunately, children born to teen parents are often denied a close connection with their father because the relationship between their parents is more likely to dissolve over time.

- Children who live apart from their fathers are five times more likely to be poor than children with both parents at home.
- Boys and girls without involved fathers are twice as likely to drop out of school, twice as likely to abuse alcohol or drugs, twice as likely to end up in jail, and nearly four times more likely to need help for emotional or behavioral problems.
- Over two decades of research confirms that parents—both fathers and mothers—are an important influence on whether their teenagers become pregnant or cause a pregnancy.

There is growing attention to the responsibilities of boys and young men in preventing teen pregnancy. At last count, 40 states had strategies to prevent unwanted or too-early fatherhood. This emphasis on primary prevention for boys and men is a welcome trend. Still, too many young men are not waiting until they are ready—emotionally and financially—to become fathers:

- The good news is that sexual activity among teenage boys is declining.
- The best available data show that after increasing 32 percent between 1986 and 1991, the teen birth rate for fathers aged 15–19 remained fairly constant until 1994, then decreased 16 percent between 1994 and 1999. These data also show that approximately 168,000 babies born to teen mothers in 1999 had fathers under age 20.
- Eight of 10 teen fathers do not marry the mothers of these children.
- Absent fathers of teen mothers pay less than $800 annually for child support, often because they are quite poor themselves.
- Some research suggests that teen fathers have lower levels of education and suffer earning losses of 10–15 percent annually than teens who do not father children.

Clearly, more needs to be done to send a strong message to teen boys and young men that they should wait to become a father until they are ready to have a lasting—ideally married—relationship to the mother of their children and are able to meet their financial and emotional responsibilities to their children. In addition, there is more that should be done to build on efforts within the teen pregnancy prevention field to reach out to boys and young men through what are sometimes called "male involvement programs." It is also important to recognize and support the important role that fathers can play in helping their own sons and daughters avoid becoming teen parents.

Teen Pregnancy and Workforce Development

Reducing teen pregnancy will strengthen the future U.S. workforce. Today's economy demands a sophisticated and educated workforce. But teen pregnancy and too-early parenthood often short circuit the education process and prevent young men and women from preparing themselves for good jobs and becoming established in the labor market.

- Teen parents and their children are less likely to graduate from high school. In fact, less than four of 10 teen mothers who begin their families before age 18 ever complete high school.
- In the past 25 years, the median income for college graduates has increased 13 percent, while median income for high school dropouts has decreased 30 percent.
- Fully half of teen mothers drop out of school *before* becoming pregnant.
- When compared to similarly situated women who delay childbearing until age 20 or 21, teen mothers and their children experience a number of adverse social and economic consequences. For example, 52 percent of all mothers on welfare had their first child as a teenager.

When children have children, their opportunities are diminished right from the start, and the future is often one of poverty. That's not good for business. The business community has a vested interest in preventing teen pregnancy and childbearing because of the associated financial, social, and workforce-related consequences. If teens can delay parenthood, they will have the time and resources they need for their education and training, which are crucial to a productive workforce in an increasingly high-tech world.

"Humans are designed to reproduce in their teens, and they're potentially very good at it. That's why they want to so much."

Teen Pregnancy Is Not a Serious Problem

Frederica Mathewes-Green

In this viewpoint Frederica Mathewes-Green argues that teens have a biological drive to reproduce and that teen pregnancy does not harm youths or society. In fact, she contends, teens are biologically and emotionally ready to have children. The author asserts that encouraging youths to wait until their twenties to have sex merely conditions them to moving in and out of multiple relationships, which leads to high divorce rates. Mathewes-Green is a regular contributor to National Public Radio's Morning Edition, *Christianity Today*, and other publications.

As you read, consider the following questions:
1. A woman's fertility begins to decline at what age, according to Mathewes-Green?
2. Are teen marriages less or more likely to end in divorce, in the author's opinion?
3. In Mathewes-Green's view, does delayed marriage mean delayed sex for teens?

True Love Waits. Wait Training. Worth Waiting For. The slogans of teen abstinence programs reveal a basic fact of human nature: teens, sex, and waiting aren't a natural combination.

Over the last 50 years the wait has gotten longer. In 1950, the average first-time bride was just over 20; in 1998 she was five years older, and her husband was pushing 27. If that June groom had launched into puberty at 12, he'd been waiting more than half his life.

If he *had* been waiting, that is. Sex is the sugar coating on the drive to reproduce, and that drive is nearly overwhelming. It's supposed to be; it's the survival engine of the human race. Fighting it means fighting a basic bodily instinct, akin to fighting thirst.

Yet despite the conflict between liberals and conservatives on nearly every topic available, this is one point on which they firmly agree: Young people absolutely must not have children. Though they disagree on means—conservatives advocate abstinence, liberals favor contraception—they shake hands on that common goal. The younger generation must not produce a younger generation.

But teen pregnancy, in itself, is not such a bad thing. By the age of 18, a young woman's body is well prepared for childbearing. Young men are equally qualified to do their part. Both may have better success at the enterprise than they would in later years, as some health risks—Cesarean section and Down Syndrome, for example—increase with passing years. (The dangers we associate with teen pregnancy, on the other hand, are behavioral, not biological: drug use, STD's [sexually transmitted diseases], prior abortion, extreme youth, and lack of prenatal care.) A woman's fertility has already begun to decline at 25—one reason the population-control crowd promotes delayed childbearing. Early childbearing also rewards a woman's health with added protection against breast cancer.

Younger moms and dads are likely [to] be more nimble at child-rearing as well, less apt to be exhausted by toddlers' perpetual motion, less creaky-in-the-joints when it's time to swing from the monkey bars. I suspect that younger parents will also be more patient with boys-will-be-boys rambunction, and less likely than weary 40-somethings to beg pediatricians for drugs to control supposed pathology. Humans are designed to reproduce in their teens, and they're potentially very good at it. That's why they want to so much.

Teen pregnancy is not the problem. *Unwed* teen pregnancy is the problem. It's childbearing outside marriage that causes all the trouble. Restore an environment that supports younger marriage, and you won't have to fight biology for a decade or more.

Most of us blanch at the thought of our children marrying under the age of 25, much less under 20. The immediate reaction is: "They're too immature." We expect teenagers to be self-centered and impulsive, incapable of shouldering the responsibilities of adulthood. But it wasn't always that way; through much of history, teen marriage and childbearing was the norm. Most of us would find our family trees dotted with many teen marriages.

Of course, those were the days when grown teens were presumed to be truly "young adults." It's hard for us to imagine such a thing today. It's not that young people are inherently incapable of responsibility—history disproves that—but that we no longer expect it. Only a few decades ago a high-school diploma was taken as proof of adulthood, or at least as a promise that the skinny kid holding it was ready to start acting like one. Many a boy went from graduation to a world of daily labor that he would not leave until he was gray; many a girl began turning a corner of a small apartment into a nursery. Expectations may have been humble, but they were achievable, and many good families were formed this way.

Hidden in that scenario is an unstated presumption that a young adult can earn enough to support a family. Over the course of history, the age of marriage has generally been bounded by puberty on the one hand, and the ability to support a family on the other. In good times, folks marry young; when prospects are poor, couples struggle and save toward their wedding day. A culture where men don't marry until 27 would normally feature elements like repeated crop failures or economic depression.

That's not the case in America today. Instead we have an

artificial situation which causes marriage to be delayed. The age that a man, or woman, can earn a reasonable income has been steadily increasing as education has been dumbed down. The condition of basic employability that used to be demonstrated by a high-school diploma now requires a bachelor's degree, and professional careers that used to be accessible with a bachelor's now require a master's degree or more. Years keep passing while kids keep trying to attain the credentials that adult earning requires.

Teen Irresponsibility Is a Myth

Financial ability isn't our only concern, however; we're convinced that young people are simply incapable of adult responsibility. We expect that they will have poor control of their impulses, be self-centered and emotional, and be incapable of visualizing consequences. (It's odd that kids thought to be too irresponsible for marriage are expected instead to practice heroic abstinence or diligent contraception.) The assumption of teen irresponsibility has broader roots than just our estimation of the nature of adolescence; it involves our very idea of the purpose of childhood.

Until a century or so ago, it was presumed that children were in training to be adults. From early years children helped keep the house or tend the family business or farm, assuming more responsibility each day. By late teens, children were ready to graduate to full adulthood, a status they received as an honor. How early this transition might begin is indicated by the number of traditional religious and social coming-of-age ceremonies that are administered at ages as young as 12 or 13.

But we no longer think of children as adults-in-progress. Childhood is no longer a training ground but a playground, and because we love our children and feel nostalgia for our own childhoods, we want them to be able to linger there as long as possible. We cultivate the idea of idyllic, carefree childhood, and as the years for education have stretched so have the bounds of that playground, so that we expect even "kids" in their mid-to-late twenties to avoid settling down. Again, it's not that people that age *couldn't* be responsible; their ancestors were. It's that anyone, offered a chance to kick back and play, will generally seize the opportunity. If our culture assumed that 50-year-olds would take a year-long break from responsibility, have all their expenses paid by someone else, spend their time having fun and making forgivable mistakes, our malls would be overrun by middle-aged delinquents.

Teen Pregnancy Is No Health Problem

There is no convincing evidence that teenage pregnancy is a public health problem and it is difficult to identify a biologically plausible reason for adverse outcomes of young maternal age . . . It makes little biological sense for young women to be able to reproduce at an age that puts their children at risk. For policy makers the labelling of teenage pregnancy as a public health problem reflects social, cultural and economic imperatives. Researchers and health practitioners should think more carefully about why something is labelled a public health problem, together with the social and moral context in which it occurs and in which they practice.

British Prime Minister Tony Blair's preface to the Social Exclusion Unit's report on teenage pregnancy indicates the strength of negative feelings:

> While the rate of teenage pregnancies has remained high here, throughout most of the rest of Western Europe it fell rapidly. As a country, we can't afford to continue to ignore this shameful record.

We do not agree that teenage pregnancy is shameful, nor do we believe that teenage pregnancy is (or is best conceptualized as) a public health problem.

Debbie A. Lawlor and Mary Shaw, *International Journal of Epidemiology*, June 2002.

But don't young marriages tend to end in divorce? If we communicate to young people that we think they're inherently incompetent that will become a self-fulfilling prophecy, but it was not always the case. In fact, in the days when people married younger, divorce was much rarer. During the last half of the 20th century, as brides' age rose from 20 to 25, the divorce rate doubled. The trend toward older, and presumptively more mature, couples didn't result in stronger marriages. Marital durability has more to do with the expectations and support of surrounding society than with the partners' age.

A pattern of late marriage may actually *increase* the rate of divorce. During that initial decade of physical adulthood, young people may not be getting married, but they're still falling in love. They fall in love, and break up, and undergo terrible pain, but find that with time they get over it. They may do this many times. Gradually, they get used to it; they learn that they can give their hearts away, and take them back again; they learn to shield their hearts from access in the first place. They learn to approach a relationship with the goal of getting what they want, and keep their bags packed by the door. By the time they marry they may have had many opportunities to learn how to walk away from a promise. They've been training for divorce.

As we know too well, a social pattern of delayed marriage doesn't mean delayed sex. In 1950, there were 14 births per thousand unmarried women; in 1998, the rate had leapt to 44. Even that astounding increase doesn't tell the whole story. In 1950 the numbers of births generally corresponded to the numbers of pregnancies, but by 1998 we must add in many more unwed pregnancies that didn't come to birth, but ended in abortion, as roughly one in four of all pregnancies do. My home city of Baltimore wins the blue ribbon for out-of-wedlock childbearing: in 2001, 77 percent of all births were to unwed mothers.

There are a number of interlocking reasons for this rise in unwed childbearing, but one factor must surely be that when the requirements presumed necessary for marriage rise too high, some people simply parachute out. It's one thing to ask fidgety kids to abstain until they finish high school at 18. When the expectation instead is to wait until 25 or 27, many will decline to wait at all. We're saddened, but no longer surprised, at girls having babies at the age of 12 or 13. Between 1940 and 1998, the rate at which girls 10–14 had their first babies almost doubled. These young moms' sexual experiences are usually classified as "non-voluntary" or "not wanted." Asking boys to wait until marriage is one way a healthy culture protects young girls.

Teen Parents Need a Support Network

The idea of returning to an era of young marriage still seems daunting, for good reason. It is not just a matter of tying the knot between dreamy-eyed 18-year-olds and tossing them out into world. Our ancestors were able to marry young because they were surrounded by a network of support enabling that step. Young people are not intrinsically incompetent, but they do still have lots of learning to do, just like newlyweds of any age. In generations past a young couple would be surrounded by family and friends who could guide and support them, not just in navigating the shoals of new marriage, but also in the practical skills of making a family work, keeping a budget, repairing a leaky roof, changing a leaky diaper.

It is not good for man to be alone; it's not good for a young couple to be isolated, either. In this era of extended education, couples who marry young will likely do so before finishing college, and that will require some sacrifices. They can't expect to "have it all." Of the three factors—living on their own, having babies, and both partners going to school full-time—something is going to have to give. But young marriage can succeed, as it always has, with the support of family and friends.

I got married a week after college graduation, and both my husband and I immediately went to graduate school. We made ends meet by working as janitors in the evenings, mopping floors and cleaning toilets. We were far from home, but our church was our home, and through the kindness of more-experienced families we had many kinds of support—in fact, all that we needed. When our first child was born we were so flooded with diapers, clothes, and gifts that our only expense was the hospital bill.

Our daughter and older son also married and started families young. Things don't come easy for those who buck the norm, but with the help of family, church, and creative college-to-work programs, both young families are making their way. Early marriage can't happen in a vacuum; it requires support from many directions, and it would be foolish to pretend the costs aren't high.

The rewards are high as well. It is wonderful to see our son and daughter blooming in strong, joyful marriages, and an unexpected joy to count a new daughter and son in our family circle. Our cup overflows with grandchildren as well:

As of [2002] we have four grandbabies, though the oldest is barely two. I'm 49.

It's interesting to think about the future. What if the oldest grandbaby also marries young, and has his first child at the age of 20? I would hold my great-grandchild at 67. There could even follow a great-great-grand at 87. I will go into old age far from lonely. My children and their children would be grown up then too, and available to surround the younger generations with many resourceful minds and loving hearts. Even more outrageous things are possible: I come from a long-lived family, some of whom went on past the age of 100. How large a family might I live to see?

Such speculation becomes dizzying—yet these daydreams are not impossible, and surely not unprecedented. Closely looped, mutually supporting generations must have been a common sight, in older days when young marriage was affirmed, and young people were allowed to do what comes naturally.

> "*Wherever adults and young people spend time together, there is a risk that an adult will pursue young people for sexual satisfaction.*"

Teen Sex with Adults Is Harmful

Michael J. Basso

Michael J. Basso is a high school teacher in Florida and a member of the American Association of Sex Educators, Counselors, and Therapists. According to Basso in the following viewpoint, adult sex with underage teens is harmful to youths. He likens it to a stronger person bullying a weaker person. He argues that teens who have sex with adults suffer a lifetime of psychological trauma.

As you read, consider the following questions:
1. In Basso's opinion, how do adults persuade teens to have sex?
2. What emotions do teens usually feel when they have had sex with an adult, according to the author?
3. Are most adults interested in having sex with teens, in Basso's view?

Michael J. Basso, *The Underground Guide to Teenage Sexuality*. Minneapolis, MN: Fairview Press, 2003. Copyright © 2003 by Michael J. Basso. All rights reserved. Reproduced by permission.

S exual contact with adults means any of the following:
- Any kind of touching, talk, or activity that an adult tries to get a young person to do or say for the adult's sexual pleasure.
- An adult who tries to get a young person to describe certain sexual acts on the telephone, over the Internet, or in person.
- An adult who asks a young person to touch him/her or creates a situation where the young person can be touched.
- An adult who wants a young person to pose naked, with very little clothes on, or in a seductive (sexually arousing) way for pictures or videos.

An Abuse of Power

What is wrong with sexual contact with adults? The same thing that is wrong with a stronger person bullying a weaker person—this is an abuse of power that can cause a lot of damage to the person who is being taken advantage of. Young people have not yet developed the skills they need to avoid being manipulated and taken advantage of by an adult who is trying to satisfy his/her sexual desires. The result is that usually a young person suffers psychological trauma that can last a lifetime. These scars can cause emotional pain and make the young person look at life or future relationships in an unhealthy and harmful way. He/She might even begin taking drugs, behaving violently, or contemplating suicide as a result.

Why do adults pursue teens for sex? There are many possible reasons why some adults want to have sexual contact with teens. People become sexually aroused by different things. Unfortunately, even though these adults know that this is very harmful to young people, they are more concerned about their own sexual desires than they are about a young person's health, life, or future.

An adult may try to get a young person to have sexual contact with him/her because the adult lacks the self-confidence to develop sexual relationships with other adults. Or such an adult believes a young person is less likely to reject him/her. Or having sex with young people makes him/

her feel powerful and in control. These are just a few of the reasons why an adult might try to have sexual contact with young people.

When it comes to adult sexual contact, what usually happens is that an adult looks for ways to have a young person satisfy his/her sexual needs without anyone finding out. He/She tries to gain the young person's trust. Once the adult has the young person's trust, it becomes easier to manipulate (trick) the young person into some kind of sexual contact, even though the young person is not romantically interested in the adult. Other times, the young person is seduced (tricked) into becoming romantically interested so she/he will engage in adult sexual contact. Either of these things can happen because a young person develops the ability to feel strong emotions like love, attraction, and guilt long before she/he develops the ability to know how to manage those emotions. This makes a person vulnerable to being manipulated.

Are there certain types of adults I should look out for? Any adult can possibly be someone who will try to take advantage of a young person. These adults come from all walks of life and have all kinds of jobs and work titles. They include business and religious leaders, counselors, teachers, principals, camp leaders, coaches, and neighbors. Never think that an adult's job title means that he/she would not take advantage of people, especially young people. Wherever adults and young people spend time together, there is a risk that an adult will pursue young people for sexual satisfaction. This puts you in a position where you must always be cautious and aware of what is happening around you. . . .

Tricking Young People

How do adults get young people to have sexual contact with them? There are many ways adults confuse, seduce, and trick young people into having sexual contact with them. They may use friendliness, humor, kindness, or understanding to gain young people's trust. They may use guilt or anger to pressure young people to engage in sexual contact. Such adults may also use gifts, compliments, money, food, or car transportation to get young people to like them or feel as though they owe them something.

Most adults *are* kind and have no interest in sexual contact with young people. The problem is that it's difficult to know whether an adult is kind and caring because he/she is interested in your well-being or because he/she wants sexual contact.

How can I tell if an adult is trying to trick me into sexual contact? At first, you probably won't know. This adult may seem like a friendly person who would never be interested in such a thing. Again, these kinds of adults might spend a lot of time trying to get to know you and gain your trust. Then, small things might begin to happen, like he/she arranges times and places for you to be alone together, or begins making inappropriate comments (sexual comments that an adult shouldn't make to a young person) or inappropriate touches (touching that an adult shouldn't have with a young person). . . .

Stopping Adult-Teen Sex

The belief that children can truly consent to sex with an adult horrifies critics across a wide spectrum. "Our major task is trying to figure out how to stop this nonsense, this justifying and encouraging adult-child sexual behavior," says Paul Fink, past president of the American Psychiatric Association.

"Is it open season on our children?" asks Stephanie Dallam, a researcher for the Leadership Council for Mental Health, Justice and the Media, a non-profit advocacy group for children that focuses on pedophilia.

The issue should not be blurred by talking about sex with a 17-year-old versus a younger child, Dallam says. "That is just one hill in the battle" pedophiles are waging, she says. "Once they have the 15- to 17-year-olds, then it will be OK with the 12- and 13-year olds."

Karen S. Peterson, *USA Today*, April 16, 2002.

An adult who is looking to have sexual contact with a young person will try to create a situation where he/she can be alone with that young person and not have to worry about another adult or person being around to see what he/she is doing. Beware of the following situations:

- An adult asking you to go to a place where there are no other adults or young people. Examples include a school room with the door closed, an adult's home, a hotel, his/her friend's house, a party (which nobody shows up for except you and that adult), and his/her car.

- An adult inviting you to watch movies/videos where there is nudity (naked people) or sex taking place.
- An adult wanting you to look at pictures, Web sites, or other materials where there are naked people or sexual situations.
- Receiving photos or pictures of naked people or pornographic material from anyone on the Internet.
- An adult showing any part of his/her genitals or who is not fully dressed.
- An adult taking you to a place where alcohol or drugs are being used.
- An adult buying food or gifts for you and then asking for "favors."
- An adult saying he/she wants to be your second Dad/Mom or your guardian angel, or who wants to be called Uncle or Aunt.
- An adult giving you rides home, to the mall, or to other places.
- Overnight sleepovers, camping trips, or field trips with an adult.
- Teachers and other school workers who offer to alter your grades or promise to keep you out of trouble.
- Receiving a raise or promotion at work ahead of people who have been there longer or who are more qualified.

Some of these situations are usually safe—like a teacher arranging time for a student to come after school to complete an assignment, a neighbor who agrees to keep an eye on a young person for Mom/Dad, and an adult mentor or club leader who drives young people places or goes on camping trips with a group of young people and adult chaperones. But if an adult makes any inappropriate sexual comments/touches in any of these situations, then this is a sign that there could be a problem.

Of course, your parent/guardian who drives you places, feeds you, gives you gifts, and takes you on vacations or trips is okay and not normally a problem.

What if an adult "comes on" to me or asks me to touch him/her? If an adult asks you out or says or does things that would indicate that he/she is interested in you sexually, then you should keep the following in mind:

- What this person is saying or trying to do is wrong and dangerous.
- What this person is saying or trying to do is not your fault at all.
- If an adult begins to touch you anywhere on your body, you should move away, or at the very least be suspicious and on the alert. If you feel uncomfortable, trust your instincts! Remove yourself from the situation immediately!
- If an adult asks you to touch his/her body, you should move away, or at the very least be suspicious and on the alert. If you feel uncomfortable, trust your instincts! Remove yourself from the situation immediately!
- You will probably feel embarrassed. This is a normal response in this type of situation. Let your parent, guardian, or other trusted adult know what happened—immediately!
- Do not meet with this adult again. Let your parent/guardian know that you are uncomfortable being with this person. Your parent/guardian should make arrangements so you do not have to be near or see this person again.
- Have your parent, guardian, or other trusted adult contact this person's boss as well as the legal authorities to investigate the situation. Chances are, if this happened to you, it may have happened or will happen to another youth just like you, except the other young person might not know how to handle it as well as you.
- Talk about what happened with a trained counselor or psychologist. Even though there may not have been any physical damage, what happened can be very scary and cause fear in the future if it isn't talked out. . . .

The Aftermath

What should I do if an adult has had sexual contact with me? You will probably feel confused, embarrassed, and afraid, or you may think that what happened was your fault. (It wasn't your fault!) You may just want to forget what happened and never mention it to anyone. These are all normal reactions, but you will need to fight these feelings and get help to prevent any further harm to yourself and to others. You need to let your parent, guardian, or other trusted adult know immediately.

The adult's abuse of you is a crime, and the event may leave a psychological scar that, if untreated, may affect your future dramatically. Your parent/guardian should contact the legal authorities, make arrangements for you never to be with or see this person again, and schedule time with a trained counselor or psychologist.

I repeat: this was not your fault. You are the victim of a crime and should have professional help in working through what happened. Some things that you should do:

- Let a trusted adult know what has happened.
- Cut off all communication with the adult who had sexual contact with you.
- Find a trained counselor to talk and release feelings with.
- If sexual intercourse took place, schedule an appointment with a doctor for pregnancy and sexually transmitted disease tests.
- Remember that the adult is to blame—always. It is never the young person's fault—ever!

Some things that you should NOT do:

- Don't keep what happened a secret.
- Don't think that the abuse will not happen again.
- Don't try to protect the adult who had sexual contact with you.
- Don't keep your feelings and thoughts about what happened to yourself.
- Don't blame yourself.

How can I prevent myself from becoming a victim of adult sexual contact? Unfortunately, anyone can be tricked or confused by an adult—even other adults! While you shouldn't be afraid of adults, you should be aware that there are some adults who look for young people to take advantage of and have sexual contact with. You should recognize the signs of an adult trying to trick a young person into having sexual contact, including inappropriate comments, touches, and situations. Remember that most adults are not interested in having sexual contact with young people and are really interested in protecting young people from those adults who are.

"Legally designating a class of people categorically unable to consent to sexual relations is not the best way to protect children, particularly when 'children' include everyone from birth to eighteen."

Teen Sex with Adults Is Not Harmful

Judith Levine

In this viewpoint Judith Levine argues that it is not harmful for teens to have sex with adults. Instead, it can be beneficial to teens, according to the author, because it makes them feel sexy, grown up, protected, and special. It also teaches them sexual skills that they would not learn from their peers, Levine writes. The author suggests that the age of consent in the United States should be lowered to 12, as it is in the Netherlands. Levine is a journalist and essayist who has written about sex, gender, and families.

As you read, consider the following questions:

1. According to Levine, what percent of adolescents age 15–17 has had some type of sex?
2. In 1800 what was the age of sexual consent in America, as reported by the author?
3. What year, according to Levine, did the Dutch parliament lower the age of consent for sex to 12?

Judith Levine, *Harmful to Minors: The Perils of Protecting Children from Sex*. New York: Thunder's Mouth Press, 2003. Copyright © 2002 by Judith Levine. Afterword copyright © 2003 by Judith Levine. Appears by permission of the publisher, Thunder's Mouth Press/Nation Books, a division of Avalon Publishing Group.

M any psychologists believe that adults' reactions even to certifiable sexual abuse can exacerbate the situation for the child, both in the short and in the long term. "There is often as much harm done to the child by the system's handling of the case as the trauma associated with the abuse," the National Center on Child Abuse and Neglect reported in 1978. But the system's handling did not appreciably improve in the next two decades, especially as criminal proceedings increased against adults in adult-minor liaisons. When the youngster has had what she considers a relationship of love and consensual sex, it does no good to tell her she has been manipulated and victimized. "To send out the message that you've been ruined for life and this person was vile and they were pretending to care—that often does a lot of damage," commented Fred Berlin, a psychiatrist at Johns Hopkins University and a well-respected expert on treating sex offenders.

How can harm be prevented rather than inflicted on youngsters? How can we even know what is harmful, so that we may be guided in guiding them toward happy and safe sexual relations?

Asking Teens About Sex

The first answer is simple, said University of Georgia social work professor Allie Kilpatrick: Ask them. Have them describe their sexual experiences, without prelabeling them as abuse. In 1992, Kilpatrick published the results of a study based on a thirty-three-page questionnaire about childhood sexual experiences, administered to 501 women from a variety of class, racial, and educational backgrounds. Instead of employing the morally and emotionally freighted phrase *sexual abuse*, she asked specific questions: How old were you, how often, with whom did you have sex? Did you initiate or did the other person? What acts did you engage in ("kiss and hug," "you show genitals," "oral sex by you," etc.)? Was it pleasurable, voluntary, coerced? How did you feel later?

Kilpatrick found that 55 percent of her respondents had had some kind of sex as children (between birth and age fourteen) and 83 percent as adolescents (age fifteen to seventeen), the vast majority of it with boys and men who were not related to them. Of these, 17 percent felt the sex was abusive, and 28 percent said it was harmful. But "the majority of young people who experience some kind of sexual behavior find it pleasurable. They initiated it and didn't feel much guilt or any harmful consequences," she told me. What about age? "My research showed that difference in age made no difference" in the women's memories of feelings during their childhood sexual experiences or in their lasting effects.

Teens often seek out sex with older people, and they do so for understandable reasons: an older person makes them feel sexy and grown up, protected and special; often the sex is better than it would be with a peer who has as little skill as they do. For some teens, a romance with an older person can feel more like salvation than victimization. Wrote Ryan, a teenager who had run away from home to live in a Minnesota commune with his adult lover, "John was the first person in my life who would let me be who I wanted to be. . . . Without John I would have been dead because I would have killed myself." Indeed, it is not uncommon for the child "victim" to consider his or her "abuser" a best friend, a fact that has led to some dicey diagnostic and criminal locutions. William Prendergast, a former prison psychologist and current frequent-flyer "expert" on child abuse, for instance, talks about "consensual rape" and young people's "pseudo-positive" sexual experiences with adults.

Of course, there are gender differences in the experiences of early sex. The law did not invent these. Boys are used to thinking of themselves as desirers and initiators of sex and resilient players who can dust themselves off from a hard knock at love. So among boys, "self-reported negative effects" of sex in childhood are "uncommon," according to psychologists Bruce Rind and Philip Tromovitch's metanalysis of national samples of people who have had such experiences. Girls and women, on the other hand, are far more often the victims of incest and rape than boys are, and gender compounds whatever age-related power imbalances an intergenerational liaison may contain. [Another study] found that girls spoke of entering such partnerships willingly and often rationally and of satisfaction with the adult status they borrowed there. Yet they also often "let their guard down with older guys," agreeing not to use a condom, to drop out of school, or cut off ties with friends and families who could have helped them after the relationship was over. Her older informants offered another vantage point from which to view such relationships, often speaking disparagingly of their past older lovers and regretfully of their choices. Phillips pointed out that such bad behavior and twenty-twenty hindsight aren't exclusive to older-younger relationships. A younger lover might have been just as unfaithful and just as likely to leave a young woman with a baby and no help.

The subjects of Sharon Thompson's *Going All the Way* represented such love affairs in far more positive ways. Just over 10 percent of the four hundred teenage girls she interviewed through the 1980s "told about actively choosing sexual experiences with men or women five or more years older than they." These girls "had no doubt that they could differentiate between abuse, coercion, and consent." They represented themselves as the aggressors, persisters, and abandoners in these relationships, adept at flipping between adult sophistication and childlike flightiness to suit their moods or romantic goals.

Which story is true—freely chosen love or sweet-talked dupery? Both, said Thompson wisely when I asked her. Phillips seemed to agree. "Rather than presuming that adult-teen relationships are *really* a form of victimization or that they *really* represent unproblematic, consensual partnerships—rather than maintaining either that willingness means consent or that an age difference means an inherent inability to consent—we need to step back and probe the nuances of adult-teen relationships from the perspectives of young women who participate in them," Phillips wrote. If we are going to educate young women to avoid potentially exploitative relationships, "those strategies must speak to [their] lived realities and the cultural and personal values that they, their families, and their communities hold regarding this issue." Phillips admitted to ambivalence about age-of-consent laws.

Historical Rise in Age of Consent

"The 'life script'—our expectations of what we will do, and do next, and next after that in life—has been greatly scrambled in U.S. and Western Europe," Teachers College education professor Nancy Lesko commented in a 2000 interview. What Americans typically believed in the 1950s—that they would go to school, then get a job, then get married, then have sex, then have children—is no longer what youngsters necessarily have in mind. "None of that is certain any longer," said Lesko. "As a result, the sense of what youth or adulthood is comes into question and needs to be redefined."

Lower Consent Age to 12

Personally, I would scrap the [British] Government's new age of consent laws. Instead, I would adopt a three-step approach. One, improve sex education. We need to empower teenagers so that they are equipped to deal with the complicated situations that sex can bring. Two, tighten laws against paedophilia. And, three, lower the age of consent to 12. Actually, I'd be open to an age-gap system such as exists in the Netherlands and Portugal. . . . Certainly, it's worthy of discussion. But, either way, I would still lower the age of consent to 12. Not because I think that teenagers should be having sex at 12, but because I think they should be delaying it until they are ready.

Twelve is an indicator, a marker between the ages of childhood and adolescence, not an average age of first sex, not the best of a bad job. Teenagers will continue to have sex when they want to, regardless of the law. What we have to do is educate them so that they don't do so until they're fully prepared. They, and we, need to talk about sex openly and without fear of prosecution. We should help them to celebrate themselves, to understand their own needs and desires. They have a right to make their own decisions about their own bodies. They have a right to enjoy sexual experimentation, if that's what they really want.

Miranda Sawyer, "Sex Is Not Just for Grown-ups." *Guardian Unlimited-Observer*, November 2, 2003. http://observer.guardian.co.uk.

Such redefinition is a subtle and never-ending task; it requires serious popular consideration and will never be settled for all time. In 1800, the age of consent was ten throughout America. In 1880, after the white-slavery panic, when a ten-year-old might be working fourteen hours a day in a factory, it was sixteen. In the 1990s, the age of consent ranged, literally, all over the map: in Hawaii in 1998 it was fourteen; in

Virginia, fifteen; Minnesota and Rhode Island, sixteen; Texas, seventeen; Wisconsin, eighteen. In New Hampshire, it was illegal for anyone to have sex with somebody under sixteen, even if both people were under sixteen.

But sex is only one marker of social majority over which the law seeks dominion. The ages at which a person can drink, smoke cigarettes, drop out of school, get an abortion without parental notification, see a violent or sexy movie, or be incarcerated in an adult prison also are in dispute, along with the question of whether parents should be held liable if their children break a law. Irrationally, as the age of sexual initiation slowly drops, the age of consent is rising. And while "adult" sex becomes a crime for minors, it is only in the area of violent criminal activity that "children" are considered fully mature: in Chicago, in the late 1990s, an eleven-year-old boy was tried for murder as an adult, and at this writing prosecutions of minors as adults are becoming almost common.

Age Doesn't Equal Maturity

There is no distinct moment at which a person is ready to take on adult responsibilities, nor is it self-evident that only those who have reached the age of majority are mature enough to be granted adult privileges. People do not grow up at sixteen, eighteen, or twenty-one, if they ever do. A three-decade study of thirty thousand adolescents and adults concluded that, cognitively and emotionally, both groups operated at an average developmental age of sixteen.

Legally designating a class of people categorically unable to consent to sexual relations is not the best way to protect children, particularly when "children" include everyone from birth to eighteen. Criminal law, which must draw unambiguous lines, is not the proper place to adjudicate family conflicts over youngsters' sexuality. If such laws are to exist, however, they must do what Phillips suggests about sexual and romantic education: balance the subjective experience and the rights of young people against the responsibility and prerogative of adults to look after their best interests, to "know better." A good model of reasonable legislation is Holland's.

The Dutch parliament in 1990 made sexual intercourse for people between twelve and sixteen legal but let them employ a statutory consent age of sixteen if they felt they were being coerced or exploited. Parents can overrule the wishes of a child under sixteen, but only if they make a convincing case to the Council for the Protection of Children that they are really acting in the child's best interest. "Through this legislation, therefore, Dutch children of 12 to 16 years accrued conditional rights of consent to sexual behaviors, and parental authority was conditionally reduced," wrote David T. Evans in *Sexual Citizenship*. "Simultaneously it was recognized that all under 16 remained open to, and thus had the right to protection from, exploitation and abuse. . . . Overall, the legal message here is that children over the age of 12 are sexual and potentially self-determining, and they remain weaker than adults, and should be protected accordingly, but not under the autonomous authority of parents."

The Dutch law, in its flexibility, reflects that late-modern script-scrambling, the hodge-podge of age and experience at the dawn of the twenty-first century. "If we admitted that we're not going to [live our lives] in the old order anymore . . . we could stop thinking of youth as deficient, as 'becoming,'" said Nancy Lesko. "We could begin to see them as capable, as knowledgeable. . . . It could be the starting point of attending to their sexuality differently."

Periodical Bibliography

The following articles have been selected to supplement the diverse views presented in this chapter.

Bill Albert
"With One Voice 2004: America's Adults and Teens Sound Off About Teen Pregnancy," December 2004. www.teenpregnancy.org.

Sawsan As-Sanie
"Pregnancy Prevention in Adolescents," *American Family Physician*, October 15, 2004.

Amy Benfer
"What's So Bad About Good Sex," April 19, 2002. www.salon.com.

Theodore Dalrymple
"A Nation of Paedophiles: If Sex with Children Is So Wicked, Why Are We Relaxed About Under-Age Pregnancy?" *New Statesman*, August 9, 2004.

Kevin Michael Grace
"Still Legal Prey at Age 14," *Report*, January 6, 2003.

William N. Grigg
"The Emancipated Child," *New American*, June 3, 2002.

Debbie A. Lawlor and Mary Shaw
"Too Much Too Young? Teenage Pregnancy Is Not a Public Health Problem," *International Journal of Epidemiology*, June 2002.

Judith Levine
"Promoting Pleasure: What's the Problem?" *SIECUS Report*, April/May 2002.

Mary Mitchell
"Underage Sex Is No Joke, Despite R. Kelly's Antics," *Chicago Sun-Times*, October 3, 2004.

Mark O'Keefe
"Some in Mainstream Contend Certain Cases of Adult-Minor Sex Should Be Acceptable," *Star Tribune*, March 26, 2002.

Karen S. Peterson
"Experts Debate Impact, Gray Areas of Adult-Child Sex," *USA Today*, April 16, 2002.

Denise Rinaldo
"Daddy Day Care: Two Years Ago, This Teen Became a Father. His Advice: 'If You Like Being a Kid, Don't Get Pregnant, and Don't Get Anybody Pregnant,'" *Scholastic Choices*, January 2004.

Miranda Sawyer
"Sex Is Not Just for Grown-Ups," *Observer*, November 2, 2003.

Kathleen Tsubata
"Q: Should Congress Be Giving More Financial Support to Abstinence-Only Sex Education? Yes: Abstinence Is Working to Decrease Teen Pregnancy and Is Building Character Among Our Nation's Youth," *Insight on the News*, November 10, 2003.

CHAPTER 3

How Should Society Respond to Teen Sex?

Chapter Preface

American society, in the form of government, has set minimum age limits on many activities that it deems unsuitable for adolescents. The age limit for drinking alcohol is 21, for smoking 18–19 (depending on the state), for gambling 18–21, and for marriage without parental consent 18, 19, or 21. Many people feel age restrictions should be placed on teen sexual activities as well. For example, many want to specify the age at which teens can consent to have sex, get abortions without parental consent or notification, and receive condoms and other forms of birth control. In addition to or in place of age limits, many activists also advocate for parental involvement in their teens' sexual decisions. Parental involvement laws are usually left up to individual states. In many states underage teens have the right to health services without their parents' consent or knowledge, including testing and treatment for sexually transmitted diseases (STDs) such as HIV.

However, the trend is toward more parental involvement. In 1999 twenty-eight states allowed underage teens to get an abortion without parental consent or notification. That number dropped to six states by 2004. Also in 1999 six states required one or both parents to be notified before a minor could obtain an abortion, and fourteen states required parental consent. Those numbers jumped to fourteen and twenty-one, respectively, by 2004. Since some states do not require parental involvement, many teens living in states with strict laws simply travel over state lines to obtain the service they want, making state parental involvement laws ineffective to some degree. In response, many advocates of such laws have worked to pass federal legislation to unify parental involvement laws. In the last few years, however, attempts by Congress to pass a federal parental involvement law have failed. The likelihood of such legislation ever passing is in question because these laws are highly controversial. In May 2005, the Supreme Court agreed to hear a New Hampshire case regarding the constitutionality of the state's parental notification law. A ruling was expected in 2006.

The National Family Planning and Reproductive Health Association takes the position that if a service at a family planning clinic requires parental involvement, some teens may be disinclined to seek other services at the clinic. If true, then young people might not obtain the counseling needed to help them avoid unwanted pregnancies. The total number of abortions could increase as a result of parental notification laws, the association states. Other teens might not seek medical attention for HIV or other STD infections, which could threaten their health. The American Academy of Pediatricians agrees: "Legislation mandating parental involvement does not achieve the intended benefit of promoting family communication, but it does increase the risk of harm to the adolescent by delaying access to appropriate medical care."

Parental involvement supporters disagree. They argue that deciding whether to have an abortion or continue a pregnancy has a major long-term impact on a young woman's psychological and emotional well-being, her ability to continue formal education, and her future financial status. Notification and consent laws help pregnant teens get support and guidance from their parents in this important decision, according to parental involvement supporters. These analysts also point out that there have been situations in which a child molester has secretly taken an underage girl to have an abortion in order to cover up his crime. Parental notification could help expose the sexual abuse. Former U.S. Senate candidate John Pinkerton, a conservative California Democrat, favors parental involvement laws. "Parents must give consent before their child can have their ears pierced or a tattoo put on," he claims. "Most voters agree that it is outrageous to allow a child to undergo any surgical procedure, let alone an invasive, irreversible procedure such as an abortion, without parental notification."

In deciding how society should respond to teen sex, experts must weigh the needs of teens with the rights of parents and the good of society. The authors in the following chapter debate the various ways society is addressing teen sexuality. Determining how autonomous a teen should be in deciding when and how to have sex is central to the debate.

> "*Society has a duty to protect underage girls from sexual exploitation by enforcing the laws against rape and statutory rape.*"

Statutory Rape Laws Should Be Enforced

Part I: Kathleen Sylvester and Jonathan O'Connell;
Part II: Dale O'Leary

In the following two-part viewpoint, Kathleen Sylvester, Jonathan O'Connell, and Dale O'Leary argue that society must protect underage teens by enforcing statutory rape laws on the books in all fifty states. In Part I Sylvester and O'Connell argue that too many teens are having sex too soon and that many of these cases constitute statutory rape. They suggest that if statutory rape laws were vigorously enforced, the number of unwed teen pregnancies might be reduced. In Part II O'Leary maintains that anyone protecting underage girls who have sex with older men should be prosecuted along with the men. Sullivan is director of and O'Connell is policy associate with the Social Policy Action Network, a conservative think tank. O'Leary is a conservative writer, educator, and pro-family activist.

As you read, consider the following questions:

1. What percent of girls under 14, according to Sylvester and O'Connell, have had sex with partners three or more years older?
2. In O'Leary's view, what negative experiences are underage girls who have sex with older men more likely to experience?

Part I: A recent startling report indicated that one out of every five children has sex before reaching age 15.

The report, produced by the National Campaign to Prevent Teen Pregnancy, also found that among sexually experienced 14-year-old girls, one in seven has been pregnant.

The report prompted worrisome newspaper headlines across the country, renewing the public debate about whether too many young people are having sex too soon.

But how should society respond?

A closer look at the numbers reveals a troubling reality about the sexual activity of some adolescent girls: Their relationships are with older male partners. The report found that 11 percent of girls under 14 have had relationships with partners three or more years older. Among minorities the numbers double: More than one-quarter of black and Hispanic girls between ages 12 and 14 reported sexual relationships with partners three or more years older.

In many cases, the relationships are criminal; they constitute statutory rape. In Maryland, a person cannot legally consent to sex until age 16. Unfortunately, laws against statutory rape are rarely enforced.

As a result, adult males take sexual advantage of teens and pre-teens every day in America, usually in plain sight, because the laws are not enforced. The girls often do not appear to be victims—they look and flirt like grown women, and many receive gifts or money. They think they know what they're getting themselves into.

But they don't.

At the least, "acting out" sexually is a sign of low self-esteem and a hunger for attention. For many troubled girls, however, sexual risk-taking is the consequence of early sexual initiation or child sexual abuse, a cause-and-effect pattern that must be recognized if they are to get the care they need.

Poverty is a factor in many statutory rape cases. The risk factors that often accompany poverty, from fragile family structure to diminished expectations and life goals, make poor girls especially vulnerable to both risky sexual behavior and exploitation in the form of unwanted sex.

Despite changing sexual values, "promiscuous girls" are still the object of derision and apathy not only from peers but also from educators and parents—the very adults who could protect them. All too often, the only adults who take notice of these girls are ones who would exploit their sexuality.

In a 1998 study from Family Planning Perspectives, 25 percent of girls reported that while their first experience with sex was not forced, it was unwanted. The younger a woman was at the age of her first sexual intercourse, the more likely she was to report it as unwanted.

Relationships between 12-, 13- and 14-year-old girls and sexually mature men are inherently unequal, often coercive and almost always damaging. In addition to the roughly 80,000 teen pregnancies resulting from these illegal relationships each year, young girls in these relationships are more likely to drop out of school, suffer from low self-esteem, become depressed, engage in delinquent or criminal behavior and become addicted to drugs or alcohol.

While most communities have ignored the problem of statutory rape because it seems too complicated to solve, some have tried to address the problem. They have developed prosecution guidelines that take into account such factors as the age gap between partners and the use of alcohol or drugs to coerce sex.

Some states use federal welfare funds to educate officials about the nature of the problem and strategies for helping young girls cope with the aftermath of these relationships. States also are trying to increase communication and trust between the social service providers who report cases and law enforcement officials who prosecute offenders. And public awareness campaigns, including Michigan's hard-hitting "Rob the Cradle and Get Yourself a Brand New Crib" slogan, have been common in recent times.

These strategies have put some men in jail and helped many young girls heal. If we wish to reduce sexual activity and pregnancy among our teen-agers, especially minority teens, we must start by acknowledging that the sexual activity in question is often a crime—and should be treated like one.

Part II: As I was waiting for the clerk to ring up my purchase my eyes fell on the "We Card" sign. I thought how far this country has come in protecting children from the dangers of smoking. When I was in high school, my school set

Age of Sexual Consent in the U.S.

- Varies from state to state, usually between 16 and 18; some states formerly forbade homosexual acts entirely, however such laws have been declared unconstitutional in 2003. Federal law forbids crossing state lines or international borders with the intent of having commercial sex with a person who is under 18, or any sex with a person who is under 16 and at least 4 years younger than the perpetrator. . . .
- Puerto Rico: 16
- Alaska, Arkansas, Connecticut, District of Columbia, Delaware, Georgia, Hawaii, Indiana, Kansas, Kentucky, Maine, Maryland, Massachusetts, Michigan, Minnesota, Mississippi, Montana, New Jersey, North Carolina, Ohio, Oklahoma, Pennsylvania, Rhode Island, South Dakota, Vermont, West Virginia: 16
- Illinois, Louisiana, Nebraska, New York, Texas: 17
- Arizona, California, North Dakota, Oregon, Tennessee, Utah, Virginia, Wisconsin: 18
- Alabama: 16
- Colorado: 15 (17 if partner 10 years older and not spouse)
- Florida: 16 (if partner under 24), 18 (all other adult partners)
- Idaho: 16 or 17 (if partner less than 5 years older), 18 (all other adult partners)
- Iowa: 14 or 15 (if partner less than 5 years older), 16 (all other adult partners)
- Missouri: 14 (if partner under 21), 17 (all other adults)
- Nevada: 14 (heterosexual), 21 (homosexual)
- New Hampshire: 16, 18 (person in position of authority)
- New Mexico: 16 (18 if partner at least 4 or more years older than minor)
- South Carolina: 14 (Under state constitution)/16 (Under state law—appears to conflict with state constitution).
- Washington: 16 (18 if partner is at least 60 months older, in a significant supervisory relationship, and uses that relationship to engage in sex with the minor).
- Wyoming: 16/18 (conflicting laws appear to set two different ages of consent)
- Military: equal to the state the base is located in if the state law is 16 yrs or greater else 16 if the state law is less that 16 yrs; homosexuality grounds for dismissal

"Age of Consent," Wikipedia.com, July 25, 2005.

up a "smoking area" so that students who smoked wouldn't do so in the lavatories.

Brain scans now prove what parents have long known, the

brains of adolescents are going through physical changes, which impair teenagers' ability to understand the consequences of their actions. Society has therefore put age restrictions on high risk activities—such as drinking, driving, smoking and sex. For example, in most states sex with a girl before her 16th birthday is a felony, even if she is willing.

In December of 2004 the National Center for Health Statistics released its report on teenage sexuality. According to the study, 26.8 percent of girls had their first sexual intercourse before age 16; for 5.7 percent of these first intercourse occurred before age 14 and of these 18.1 percent said the intercourse was not voluntary and 36.5 percent of their first male partners were 4 or more years older.

Underage girls who have sex with older men are more likely to experience negative outcomes. They are more likely to become pregnant, to drop out of school, to abuse drugs or alcohol, to be lured into prostitution, to end up on welfare, to be victims of domestic violence, or attempt suicide. They also have more sexual partners over time, which exposes them to a greater risk of contracting an STD [sexually transmitted disease].

We are currently in the midst of a pandemic of sexually transmitted diseases. In 2000, 9 million cases of STDs were reported among persons 15–24. While condoms are touted as the solution, they provide little or no protection against cancer-causing human papilloma virus, incurable herpes or infertility-causing gonorrhea.

Society has a duty to protect underage girls from sexual exploitation by enforcing the laws against rape and statutory rape. The goal of such enforcement would not be to fill the jails, but put fear into the hearts of males who see underage girls as easy targets. The [perpetrator] should not be rewarded because his seduction was successful. Unwillingness on the part of the girl to testify because she thinks she's "in love" should not prevent prosecution. DNA evidence can determine the perp's identity.

Current sex education programs focus on teaching girls to say "no" or, worse, negotiate "safe sex." Prosecuting statutory rape would send a strong message to every male; even if he can seduce an underage girl into saying "yes," he can be charged with a felony.

Nor should the perp get off by claiming the girl initiated the activity. Men need to understand that if a girl has not reached the age of consent, it doesn't matter what she does or says, legally she cannot consent. Men should be so afraid of being prosecuted for rape or statutory rape that they start demanding to see a woman's ID before they engage in any sexual activity—a sexual "I card" policy.

But prosecuting the men is not enough. We also need to go after those who cover up the crime—doctors, school counselors and, most of all, abortion providers. If an underage girl is pregnant or infected with an STD, a crime has been committed. To treat that girl without reporting the crime and send her back into the same situation constitutes conspiracy with the felon and should be against the law.

And what about the attorneys who help underage girls get a judge's approval of an abortion without parental notification? These lawyers and these judges should be forced to turn the evidence over to the police and the police should be forced to investigate and prosecute.

Some jurisdictions are attempting to protect girls. Against this, however, the abortion advocates are fighting to protect their business. When Kansas Attorney General Phill Kline sought records from abortion clinics in order to enforce Kansas laws against sex with girls under 14, the abortion clinics got an injunction to prevent him from looking at the files of underage girls who had abortions.

Mark Crutcher of Life Dynamics tested 800 abortion providers to see how they would react when a girl called, claiming to be 13 and pregnant by a 21 year old man, and asked if her abortion would be secret. In the vast majority of cases the person at the abortion clinic answering the phone informed the girl that her "boyfriend" was at risk for being arrested and then gave her instructions on how to conceal her and his age when she came in for her abortion.

If half as much energy went into preventing the sexual victimization of underage girls as presently goes into preventing smoking, we would see dramatic changes in the physical and emotional health of our most vulnerable young women. But this won't happen until the public becomes outraged.

| "*Supporters of tougher enforcement of statutory rape laws rarely acknowledge that such a policy may jeopardize relationships between . . . these men and their children.*"

Enforcing Statutory Rape Laws Will Not Prevent Teenage Pregnancy

Patricia Donovan

Statutory rape laws make it a crime for an adult to have sex with a minor. In the following viewpoint Patricia Donovan argues that enforcing statutory rape laws may actually harm young women and their children. According to Donovan, most young people are not aware of such laws, thus the statutes cannot affect an adult man's decision to have sex with a minor. Moreover, by making men who have sex with their minor girlfriends eligible for prosecution, the law discourages them from coming forward with support when their partners get pregnant. Patricia Donovan is a contributing editor for *Family Planning Perspectives* and senior associate for law and public policy at the Alan Guttmacher Institute in Washington, D.C.

As you read, consider the following questions:

1. How did statutory rape laws become part of the American legal system, as explained by the author?
2. According to Donovan, what steps has California taken to increase enforcement of its statutory rape laws?

Patricia Donovan, "Can Statutory Rape Laws Be Effective in Preventing Adolescent Pregnancy?" *Family Planning Perspectives*, vol. 29, 1997, pp. 30–34, 40. Copyright © 1997 by the Alan Guttmacher Institute. Reproduced by permission.

Studies indicate that at least half of all babies born to minor women are fathered by adult men. In addition, there is a widespread perception that these young mothers account for the large increase in welfare caseloads over the last 25 years. As a result, a growing number of policymakers are embracing the notion that adolescent pregnancy rates can be lowered and welfare costs reduced if states more rigorously enforce statutory rape laws prohibiting sexual intercourse between adults and minors.

In 1996, several states have taken steps to punish men who violate these laws. Meanwhile, the new federal welfare law urges that "states and local jurisdictions . . . aggressively enforce statutory rape laws" and requires state welfare plans to outline an education and training program for law enforcement officials, counselors and educators that focuses on "the problem of statutory rape." It also directs the attorney general to implement a program to study the connection between statutory rape and adolescent pregnancy, with particular attention to "predatory older men."

Protecting Young Women

Concerns about statutory rape are particularly acute in regard to the youngest adolescents. Although relatively small proportions of 13–14-year-olds have had intercourse,[1] those who become sexually active at an early age are especially likely to have experienced coercive sex: Seventy-four percent of women who had intercourse before age 14 and 60% of those who had sex before age 15 report having had a forced sexual experience. As policymakers and the public have become increasingly aware that the sexual partners of minor adolescent women are often not adolescents themselves but men 3–6 years older, concern has grown that protective measures, in the form of increasing enforcement of statutory rape laws, are necessary to guard these young women from abuse and exploitation.

The new focus on statutory rape laws, which have been on the books in every state for decades but have been largely ig-

1. Seven percent of adolescent females have had intercourse by age 13, 13% have done so by age 14, and 19% have had intercourse by age 15.

nored, has prompted public debate over the effectiveness of this approach as a potential remedy for the ongoing problem of adolescent pregnancy and childbearing. Advocates of tougher enforcement assert that adult men who "prey" on minor women will avoid these involvements if they believe that prosecution and severe punishment will follow violation of the law. The result, these advocates predict, will be fewer adolescent pregnancies and births, and, therefore, lower state and federal expenditures for welfare and health care benefits.

Most experts, however, do not believe that greater enforcement of statutory rape laws can significantly reduce adolescent pregnancy and birth rates. As DePaul University associate law professor Michelle Oberman observes, statutory rape laws are probably necessary because "minor girls are . . . uniquely vulnerable to coercion and exploitation in their sexual decision-making." At the same time, she notes, "drawing a connection between enforcing these laws and lowering adolescent pregnancy rates flies in the face of everything we know about why girls get pregnant and why they choose to continue their pregnancies. The problem is much more complicated than simply older men preying on younger women." As Oberman and others observe, adolescent child-bearing is the result of an intricate web of factors, including limited opportunity, entrenched poverty, low self-esteem and many other issues that statutory rape laws do not address.

Interviews conducted with law enforcement officials, reproductive health care providers, women's rights activists and policy analysts in the summer and fall of 1996 found advocates of tougher enforcement of statutory rape laws suggesting that such an approach is a worthwhile strategy to consider, even if it turns out to have little or no effect on adolescent pregnancy and birth rates. Others warned that a concerted effort to prosecute statutory rape cases could in fact have an adverse impact. Many providers, for example, cautioned that such efforts could discourage some teenagers from obtaining reproductive health care, for fear that disclosing information about their partners could lead to a statutory rape charge and the man's incarceration. Moreover, statutory rape prosecutions could jeopardize the support that young mothers receive from their partners, and could make it less likely that these men would develop relationships with their children.

How Statutory Rape Laws Came About

Statutory rape laws are based on the premise that until a person reaches a certain age, that individual is legally incapable of consenting to sexual intercourse. Statutory rape was codified into English law more than 700 years ago, when it became illegal "to ravish," with or without her consent, a "maiden" under the age of 12. In 1576, the age of consent was lowered to 10.

Statutory rape laws became part of the American legal system through English common law. As in England, early lawmakers in this country adopted 10 as the age of consent. However, during the 19th century, states gradually raised the age of consent, in some cases to 21. Today, the age of consent ranges from 14 to 18 years of age; in more than half of the states, the age of consent is 16.

While all states prohibit sexual activity between adults and minors in at least some circumstances, the laws vary enormously from state to state. Most statutes do not refer specifically to statutory rape; instead, they use designations such as sexual abuse, sexual assault, unlawful sexual conduct or carnal knowledge to identify prohibited activity. Most states have classifications and degrees of criminal behavior based on the age of the victim and the age difference between the victim and the "perpetrator."

Laws on the Books Versus Laws in Action

Until recently, statutory rape laws applied exclusively to females, reflecting the long-held view that only girls and young women were so vulnerable as to warrant special protection. Today, however, most laws are gender neutral. Statutory rape laws were originally intended to protect the chastity of young women, and even today, many states allow defendants to argue that a minor who is already sexually experienced does not merit the protection of statutory rape laws. A few states also permit a defendant to claim that he or she mistakenly believed that the minor was older than was actually the case.

Statutory rape law is an area in which "the law on the books . . . differs markedly from the law in action." For example, data from the period 1975–1978 (gathered for a case argued before the Supreme Court) indicate that, on average, only 413 men were arrested annually for statutory rape in California, even though 50,000 pregnancies occurred among underage women in 1976 alone.

A major reason for the dearth of cases is that statutory rape is difficult to prosecute. The young women involved are often unreliable, hostile witnesses who change or deny their story on the witness stand. "They don't want to go into court and talk about sex," observes Kathleen Sylvester, vice president of the Progressive Policy Institute, which is cosponsoring with the American Bar Association a major study of states' enforcement of statutory rape laws.

Enforcing the Law

California has begun a concerted effort to use its statutory rape laws as a means of reducing pregnancies and births among minors. The attempt was prompted by 1996 research indicating that two-thirds of babies born to school-aged mothers in the state were fathered by adult men, who, on average, were more than four years older than their adolescent partners.

"One of the most disturbing things about [the] exploding [rate of] teen pregnancy is that so many of the fathers are . . . men, 26 and 28 years old, having sex with 14-year-old girls," declared California Gov. Pete Wilson. "We've got to enforce statutory rape laws."

In fall 1995, [then] Governor Wilson announced a plan allocating $2.4 million of the state's adolescent pregnancy prevention funds to support prosecution of statutory rape cases. The plan, known as the Statutory Rape Vertical Prosecution Program, provides funding to hire additional personnel to work exclusively on statutory rape cases and allows the same prosecutor and investigator to remain on a case from beginning to end. According to Governor Wilson, vertical prosecution leads to higher conviction rates by fostering cooperation from victims and witnesses (who get to know the prosecutors) and permitting close communication between attorneys and law enforcement officials. The Governor predicted that "the increased ability to more aggressively prosecute statutory rape offenders will send a loud message that there will be serious consequences for adult men who impregnate minors, thereby creating a significant deterrent effect."

Initially, the 16 California counties with the highest rates of adolescent pregnancy involving adult men each received $150,000 to hire new staff. Early in 1996, however, the governor proposed a $6 million expansion of the initiative—bringing the total allocated to $8.4 million—to fund the state's remaining counties.

In addition to increased criminal prosecution, statutory rape offenders in California also face civil penalties under legislation enacted in September 1996. The "Teenage Pregnancy Prevention Act of 1995" provides for liabilities ranging from $2,000–$25,000, depending on the difference in the partners' ages. The statute claims that "illicit sexual activity between adult males and teenage . . . girls" has resulted in the state having the country's highest adolescent pregnancy and birth rates and spending billions of dollars annually to provide welfare and health care benefits to families headed by adolescents.

Several other states have also moved to identify and punish "male predators," the term often used by politicians and the media to describe adult men who have sex with minors. Delaware, for example, enacted the "Sexual Predator Act of 1996," which doubles the penalty for adults convicted of having sex with adolescents who are 10 or more years younger than themselves and increases the sentence for adults who have intercourse with minors younger than 14. "We will be investigating and prosecuting these abuse cases to the fullest extent possible," declared Governor Thomas Carper.

Delaware has also begun stationing state police in high schools to identify students who have become involved with adult men. "If we are committed to ensuring that our welfare reform and teen pregnancy prevention efforts are successful, we must recognize that older men frequently prey on young, vulnerable girls," the governor said. "Those officers have strong ties to the students and to the community, making them valuable allies in the effort to identify and investigate cases where girls are being victimized by adult men."

Meanwhile, Georgia raised its age of consent from 14 to 16 and increased to 10 years the minimum prison sentence for men aged 21 and older convicted of statutory rape. Florida voted in 1996 to make impregnation of a minor younger than age 16 by a male aged 21 or older a reportable form of child abuse. It also toughened its statutory rape law to prohibit sexual intercourse between a person aged 24 or older and a minor aged 16 or 17. (The law formerly stated that it was illegal for anyone to have sex with a person "of previous chaste character" younger than 18.)

"The specific problem we are trying to attack is older men preying on younger girls," explained State Senator Locke Burt, a cosponsor of the measure. Legislators in other states, including Pennsylvania and Texas, are also considering options for discouraging sexual activity between adolescent women and adult men.

How the Law Will Work

Some advocates of more diligent enforcement of statutory rape laws believe that incarceration of men who are convicted of the crime will by itself have an impact on teenage pregnancy and birth rates. "We hope to remove from the streets many of these men, a number of whom are multiple offenders," says Michael Carrington, deputy director of California's Office of Criminal Justice Planning, which administers the vertical prosecution program. "To the degree that they are out of the picture, the potential for adolescent pregnancy will be reduced."

A more common view is that adult men will be deterred from getting involved with minor women in the first place if a state makes clear its intention to vigorously prosecute statutory rape and follows through on that threat with some highly publicized cases. "When we prosecute a few of these guys, we think it'll make a lot of guys think twice," predicts Jim Hollman, deputy district attorney in California's Tulare County.

Garrett Randall, deputy district attorney in San Diego County, who has prosecuted more than two dozen cases and has won 19 convictions as of January 1, 1997, says that it is already happening in his area. "The idea that sex with young females is against the law and the law is being enforced is spreading here," he reports. (In 1997, Randall's office is prosecuting only cases in which a pregnancy has occurred and the man is at least six years older than the underage woman.)

The enforcement strategy is only likely to act as a deterrent, however, if the men it targets—and their young partners—know that these relationships are illegal. Indeed, law enforcement officials and health care providers have different perceptions of the public's knowledge of the issue. "Predators know they are not supposed to have sex with someone who is underage," asserts Rick Trunfio, an assistant district attorney in Syracuse, New York.

"The perpetrators know," agrees Carrington of California's Office of Criminal Justice Planning. "They may not know all the legal definitions and precise sentences for different age ranges, but they know they have been able to get away with a crime."

In contrast, reproductive health care providers say that clients and their partners often know little or nothing about statutory rape. "Very few know the rules," reports Margie Fites Siegle, executive director of the Los Angeles Regional Family Planning Council. According to Sylvia Ivy, executive director of The Help Everyone (THE) Clinic in Los Angeles, "Patients don't use terms like statutory rape, or even rape, to describe sexual relationships that to others might sound like rape."

Problems with the Law

Law enforcement officials appear to see no harm in implementing a strategy whose effectiveness is unknown. According to San Diego prosecutor Randall, lack of evidence that enforcing statutory rape laws will lower adolescent pregnancy rates is "not a good reason not to try it."

In contrast, many reproductive health care providers believe there are good reasons not to pursue this strategy. Such an approach could exacerbate more problems than it would solve; providers are especially worried that publicity about statutory rape prosecutions will discourage pregnant and sexually active adolescents from seeking medical care for fear of having to reveal the identity and age of their partners. "I'm concerned that we'll have a situation in which women will not be comfortable disclosing information to their health care provider," says Siegle.

Providers point out that a young woman might be unlikely to jeopardize a relationship with a man whom she loves or from whom she receives support. Furthermore, they note, an adolescent might fear physical abuse in retribution for reporting a man to authorities. Teenagers are likely "to shut down" in such situations, says Amy Coen, executive director of the Planned Parenthood Association [a national organization that provides information about sexuality and reproduction] of the Chicago Area. "They won't seek help or, if they do, they won't tell the truth." In either case, Coen adds, "you cut off an avenue of [emotional] support."

Providers also point out that in some cultures it is accepted, even encouraged, for young girls to have relationships with much older men. Indeed, a family may promise their young daughter to a much older man, in part because he will help support the entire family. These cultural practices are "not going to change by throwing people in jail," observes Catherine Wiley, family planning director of the John Wesley Community Health Institute, a large community-based health center in Los Angeles. California officials acknowledge that cultural sensitivities are an issue in some circumstances, but say that taxpayers should not have to pay for these practices in the form of welfare and health benefits for adolescent mothers and their children fathered by adult men.

A Conflict of Interest

No state currently requires reproductive health care providers to gather and report information on the identity and age of their adolescent clients' sexual partners (unless they have reason to suspect a young woman has been abused). Providers say they do not routinely collect such information. "Trust is an important part of our relationship with patients," notes Ivy of THE Clinic. "If adolescents are communicating honestly with us about a partner and it turns out that he is an adult, a requirement to report the relationship as statutory rape would place clinics in a very awkward position; we would be used by law enforcement officials for goals they've determined to be in the public's interest, but which may not be in the patient's best interest. We want to be law-abiding, but we don't want to turn ourselves into an arm of the law."

Peggy Romberg, executive director of the Texas Family Planning Association, shares Ivy's concerns: "Mandatory reporting would place family planning providers in a terrible bind. We don't want the reputation that we're not a safe haven for counseling and services." On the other hand, she adds, clinics cannot afford to have employees arrested for failure to report suspected cases of statutory rape.

Such concerns are reflected in the Florida legislature's decision to exempt certain providers from a reporting requirement in the state's recently enacted law on child abuse. It requires that "known or suspected child abuse involving impregnation of a child under 16 years of age by a person 21 years of age or older . . . [be reported] immediately to the appropriate county sheriff's office or other appropriate law enforcement agency." The requirements do not apply, though, to "health care professionals or other persons who provide medical or counseling services to pregnant children when such reporting would interfere with the provision of medical services." One of the bill's sponsors acknowledges that at least some supporters did not want health care professionals "to turn into police officers."

The Consequences on Fathers

Sponsors of programs designed to encourage men's involvement with their partners and children are also concerned about the consequences of mandatory reporting. Having to identify program participants who are adult men known to be involved with underage mothers would hamper their ability to enlist men into their programs. "There is a lot of concern about being put in a situation of having to report dads or would-be dads with adolescent partners," reports Jane Boggess, chief of California's office of family planning.

Advocates of more stringent enforcement of statutory rape laws have apparently ignored the philosophical conflict between these laws and existing statutes authorizing minors to consent to various types of reproductive health care, such as contraceptive services, screening and treatment for sexually transmitted diseases (STDs) and prenatal care. In Georgia, for example, where the legislature recently raised the age of consent for sexual intercourse to 16, state law authorizes minors to consent to STD testing and treatment, but some health officials have suggested that a statutory rape investigation be initiated whenever an underage female seeks STD services.

Such a policy, says state epidemiologist Kathleen Toomey, would "not only discourage kids from seeking care, undermining many of our prevention efforts, but it would deter providers from reporting cases, making it even harder for us to obtain reliable data on STDs."

Supporters of tougher enforcement of statutory rape laws rarely acknowledge that such a policy may jeopardize relationships between adolescent mothers and their partners, and between these men and their children. These advocates frequently portray the men they seek to prosecute as irresponsible and predatory, interested in pursuing relationships with adolescents solely to engage in sex with minors. While this may accurately describe some individuals, other adult men who father the children of adolescent women play an important role in the lives of their offspring. Professionals who work with pregnant and parenting adolescents report that young mothers often receive crucial support in the form of cash, baby products and household goods from their baby's father.

"Adult [men] impregnating teenage girls is a troublesome phenomenon that is . . . unacceptable, . . . but we have to be very careful here," warns Lois Salisbury, executive director of Children Now, an advocacy group in Oakland, California. "We're talking about someone who has a baby to raise, and she needs resources to help raise that baby and she needs a father to help raise that baby. I don't see where it's human logic or nature that would motivate her to send that father to jail."

Coen, of Chicago Planned Parenthood, agrees. "Nobody is talking about the baby. If these young women are going to have these babies, I would like them to have some support in their lives."

Andrew Doniger, director of the Monroe County Health Department in New York (which has put up more than 100 billboards warning men that it is a crime to have sex with women younger than 17), adds that "if we drive a wedge between the father and the mother, it could make things worse for the youngsters."

In fact, the support of these adult men can be so important that welfare case workers in at least one California county have on several occasions recommended—and the courts have agreed—that an underage pregnant adolescent marry her adult partner (including a 13-year-old whose partner was 20). "We do this in those few cases in which it seems best for the girl and the child," explains Larry M. Leaman, director of the Orange County Social Services Agency. These are "cases where we have a man who is standing by the teenage mother, wanting to do the right thing, ready for a family, willing to support it and where the girl's parents, if they are around, also favor the marriage." (The agency's willingness to recommend marriage is highly controversial, and Leaman has ordered a review of the agency's handling of these cases.)

Dubious Advantages

The strict enforcement of statutory rape laws is the latest in a series of punitive measures that states have adopted recently in an attempt to force people to change their sexual and reproductive behavior. There has been considerable doubt as to whether other such proposals (e.g., the so-called family cap, which denies additional cash benefits to women who bear children while on welfare) will achieve their stated objectives—lower birthrates among women likely to require public assistance and reduced welfare caseloads and costs. Likewise, there is widespread skepticism as to whether the use of statutory rape laws will have a noticeable effect on adolescent pregnancy and birth rates or on the number of young women who have sexual relationships with adult men.

One has only to look at the statistics from California to understand these doubts. In the first 11 months of the state's vertical prosecution program, 617 statutory rape cases were filed statewide, of which 293 resulted in convictions. (Others are still pending.) While these numbers will surely rise in the wake of the program's recent expansion, the program is almost certain to address only a tiny fraction of the potential cases. In 1993 alone, for example, it is estimated that more than 30,000 underage adolescents in the state gave birth to a baby fathered by an adult man. Even Carrington of the Office of Criminal Justice Planning concedes that the impact of the vertical prosecution program will be "small, given the resources applied, compared with the gravity of the problem."

Michael Males, a University of California researcher, documented the extent of adult male involvement in births among California adolescents. He and other observers believe that the current focus on statutory rape reflects the frustration of politicians searching for "a simple solution" to the continuing problem of adolescent pregnancy and childbearing, rather than concern for the well-being of young adolescents.

"People are so eager to blame one cause so the situation can be fixed, "comments Mary Margaret Wilson, who is with the New York Council on Adolescent Pregnancy. "I'm scared people are going to say, 'Aha! This is why there is adolescent pregnancy. If we just get teens to name the perpetrators and their ages, the problem will go away.' People don't want to look at bigger things like poverty and racism."

Indeed, an overwhelming majority of young women who become pregnant and give birth are from poor or low-income families. Most lack access to good schools, face poor prospects for finding jobs and have little chance of marriage. As a result, many see little reason to avoid pregnancy and to postpone childbearing.

Not All Fathers Are Predators

Moreover, while public debate over the use of statutory rape laws to prevent adolescent pregnancies has been framed largely in terms of so-called predatory older men who seek out young girls, the data suggest that these relationships, account for only a slight fraction of adolescent births. In California, for example, fewer than 3% of all teenage births are to women younger than 15 (median age for this group is approximately 14.5); of these, nearly two-thirds are fathered by men 19 or younger. Among adolescent mothers aged 15–17 whose partner is an adult male, the women's median age is 17.1, while that of their partner is 21.4.

Additionally, providers say that it is not uncommon for adolescent women to pursue adult men. Adult men are more likely than adolescents to have a job, a car and money to spend. The accoutrements that adult men can provide "are an appealing beacon in the dark" for disadvantaged adolescents, observes Wilson. That is not likely to change until young women have access to good schools and jobs and develop a sense that their lives can improve.

"I think politicians have it backwards," concludes Valerie Small Navarro, a lobbyist for the California Civil Liberties Union. "They think you can slap a criminal penalty on the problem and the problem will go away." To reduce adolescent pregnancies, Navarro contends, "they have to be willing to invest time and money in women, not incarcerate men."

> *"Parental consent laws exist as safeguards to protect young girls from making a lifelong decision without the wise counsel of their parents."*

States Should Enforce Parental Consent Laws

James C. Lesnett Jr. and Stephen Daniels

State parental consent laws require that one or both parents of a minor give approval before the girl can have an abortion. In this viewpoint James C. Lesnett Jr. and Stephen Daniels maintain that parental notification laws for teen abortions are needed because parents offer wise guidance. They also note that parents must give consent for other medical procedures, including body piercing and receiving aspirin at school. The authors argue that parental consent laws should be enforced in states that already have them. Lesnett served as a legal intern with the North Carolina Family Policy Council (NCFPC) in 2002. Daniels is director of research for NCFPC.

As you read, consider the following questions:
1. How many states, as of August 2002, have parental consent or notification laws, according to Lesnett and Daniels?
2. In the authors' view, what has the U.S. Supreme Court ruled must be in any parental involvement law?
3. The debate over parental consent is an extension of the debate over what issue, write the authors?

S hould the law require parents to give consent before their teenage daughter has an abortion? In a country where the abortion controversy has polarized much of the nation into two opposing camps, the answer is an overwhelming yes.

Parental consent for abortion laws do not seek to undermine the current legal protections for abortion. Instead, they simply reinforce the widely accepted and fundamental principle that parents should be involved in any decision related to their own children, including those that involve an invasive surgery that carries with it potential medical and psychological risks. These laws are also a common sense way to ensure that young girls who may be facing a very difficult and potentially life changing decision do not undergo this medical procedure uninformed and without the counsel of their parents.

Parental consent and parental notification laws are both designed to encourage parental involvement in the abortion decision, but each has different requirements. Parental consent laws require that a parent and the child consent to the abortion before it can be given. In addition, several states require the consent of both parents before an abortion can be legally performed. In contrast, parental notification laws merely require that the parents be notified before or after the abortion takes place, but their consent to the procedure is not necessary.

Currently forty-two states, including North Carolina, have statutes on the books that require parental consent or notification. However, only thirty-two states have laws that are actually in effect. New Mexico does not enforce the law, and in nine other states, parental consent or notification laws are not in effect because they are under court injunction.

North Carolina's parental consent law is in effect and is being enforced; however, a 1997 court ruling created an unfortunate loophole that has greatly weakened the law. . . .

Why Parental Consent?

Parental consent requirements are not unique to the abortion issue. Parents must give consent for other medical procedures (excluding emergencies), including matters such as ear piercing or receiving aspirin at school. In light of this fact, it is odd that parental consent is not required in all states, considering the risks that the abortion procedure carries with it. No one would ever want a minor to have any major medical procedure without the permission of a parent. Imagine if a doctor decided to remove a child's tonsils without first gaining the parent's permission, there would be a justified outcry from the parents and the medical community. It is reasonable to expect that the same common sense parental consent measures that apply to every other medical procedure, should also apply to abortion.

The decision of whether or not to have an abortion could undoubtedly affect a teenager's short and long term physical, mental and emotional health. Therefore, it seems common sense would dictate that teens would need adult counseling in making this decision. And most would assume that this responsibility would naturally fall to the parents. So why, with all of these risks, is abortion so often granted protected status? It is because, to many, the issue is no longer a matter of health, but it has become mired in a political agenda.

Opponents sometimes argue that these laws may be unconstitutional because they regulate a woman's right to an abortion. However, this argument ignores the multitude of rulings to the contrary. Even in the infamous *Roe v. Wade* case, the Supreme Court did not say that the right to abortion was absolute. The court took into consideration the competing interests of privacy and state involvement. Throughout the decades since then, the Supreme Court has consistently ruled that parental consent or notification laws are constitutional as long as they contain a judicial bypass.

The same has been found true of North Carolina's parental consent law. In 1997, the Fourth Circuit Court of Appeals found in *Manning v. Hunt*, that the state's law was constitutional and did not violate a woman's right to an abortion. According to the ruling, North Carolina's law passes constitutional muster because it would allow a minor to bypass her parent's consent and appeal to a judge if necessary.

Despite the political rhetoric, parental consent laws exist as safeguards to protect young girls from making a lifelong decision without the wise counsel of their parents. They are not, as some claim, a veiled attempt to undo the current legal safeguards for abortion.

The Medical Risks of Abortion

In defending the right of women to have an abortion, advocates proceed on the premise that abortion is a safe procedure. However, study after study has shown that this is far from the truth. In fact, the results reveal that abortion is a very dangerous procedure because of its harmful physical and psychological effects. Over one hundred physical problems have been associated with abortion including infections, bleeding, fevers, chronic abdominal pain, gastrointestinal disturbances, vomiting, ripping of the uterus, and hemorrhaging. Abortion can result in infertility and even death. Abortion has also been associated with severe psychological problems such as depression, drug abuse, sleep disorders, sexual dysfunction, flashbacks, and increased tendency to attempt suicide. Unfortunately, teenagers are at an especially high risk of having these physical and psychological problems.

With these risks in mind, it is difficult to classify any abortion as an innocuous medical procedure, especially when a minor is the one having it. Therefore, the decision to have an abortion must be made within the confines of the family.

Abortion clinics profit financially from each abortion they perform. In fact, for many clinics, this is the only "service" they provide. Planned Parenthood Federation of America (which performs about 15 percent of all abortions in the U.S.) made $69 million in income from abortions in the year 2000. It has been estimated that Planned Parenthood has made over $815 million from abortions since 1977. Obviously, groups like this have a financial and ideological incentive for keeping abortion legal and readily available, because if these procedures stop, the abortion industry and the income it generates, would suffer.

To protect its business, the industry has not provided complete information about abortion. To the contrary, studies have shown that women do not receive adequate counseling prior to an abortion. One study found that 90 percent of women surveyed felt they did not have enough information to make an informed decision. Almost 80 percent of women surveyed believed they were misinformed or denied relevant information during their pre-abortion counseling. If women do not believe they are being given enough information, it is likely that vulnerable and confused young girls are also not getting the information they need to make an informed decision. Thus, it is important that the parents be able to participate in their daughter's decision-making process and to ensure that she has wise counsel before making up her mind. Leaving the counseling to the abortion clinics, whose interest lie in supporting their own industry, presents a clear conflict of interest.

It is also crucial that the parent—not just another friendly adult—be the one who consents to a teen's abortion. Parents are in the best position to provide the doctor with the medical history of the teen, and this information could be important in weighing the possibility of complications. If an abortion is performed, parents who have knowledge of this fact can be sure that the teen receives the appropriate medical care if there are complications. Parents are also likely responsible for any medical bills that may result from any abortion complication, so it would seem only fair to make them aware of this possibility beforehand.

A Risk to Youth?

Opponents of parental involvement laws frequently claim that these laws force teenagers to have illegal abortions rather than risk telling their parents. Although no statistical evidence is given to prove this claim, opponents often cite a 17 year-old Indiana teenager named Becky Bell, who many abortion supporters claim died from an illegal abortion after Indiana passed a parental consent law. However, according to the autopsy, Becky Bell did not die of an abortion, but instead had a miscarriage and later died of pneumonia. Despite this fact, abortion advocates such as the ACLU [American Civil Liberties Union] and NARAL [National Association to Reform Abortion Laws] continue to mislead the public about this tragic death. In truth, parental consent laws do not force young women into abortions. Instead, the Becky Bell case reinforces the view that these young women need a safeguard in place to insure that they do not seek an abortion without first consulting their parents.

Another common argument made by those who oppose

Support for Parental Involvement

- *Religious support:* Essentially all Fundamentalist and other Evangelical religious denominations are believed to support parental involvement laws.

- *Parental rights:* Parents have the right to know about any significant activity of their under-age teens. Senatorial candidate John Pinkerton (D-CA) comments: "Parents must give consent before their child can have their ears pierced or a tattoo put on. In fact, in public schools and emergency rooms, parents must give consent before their child can be treated with so much as an aspirin. Most voters agree that it is outrageous to allow a child to undergo any surgical procedure, let alone an invasive, irreversible procedure such as an abortion, without parental notification."

- *Welfare of the Child:* Deciding whether to have an abortion or continue the pregnancy will probably have a major long-term impact on the woman's psychological and emotional well-being, her ability to continue formal education, her future financial status, etc. Notification and consent laws help pregnant teens get support and guidance from their parents in this important decision. California state attorneys stated in a brief: "To deny parents the opportunity . . . risks or perpetuates estrangement or alienation from the child when she is in the greatest need of parental guidance and support and denies all dignity to the family."

- *Safety:* A woman who has an abortion in secret, and experiences complications may be disinclined to reveal the problem to her parents. Complications, while rare, could conceivably develop to threaten the woman's life.

- *Criminal activity:* There have been situations in which a child molester has secretly taken an under-aged girl to have an abortion, in order to cover up his crime. Parental notification could help expose the sexual abuse.

Bruce A. Robinson, "Parental Consent/Notification for Teen Abortions: Pros and Cons." Religious Tolerance, April 28, 2005. www.religious tolerance.org.

---

parental involvement laws is that they could lead to abuse by angry parents or endanger teens that have been victimized by incest or rape at the hands of a family member. This argument ignores the fact that the U.S. Supreme Court has ruled that a judicial bypass must be included in any parental involvement law for just these reasons. A minor who cannot obtain consent or does not want to ask for it may ask a judge, in a confidential hearing, to grant a bypass by taking into consideration factors such as maturity and the best interests of the teen.

Throughout history, parents have always been considered the rightful guardians of the future and well-being of their children. More than anyone else, parents have a vested interest in their child's success and good health. In order to ensure such things, parents must have the discretion to make choices that are in their child's best interest. This is relevant to any medical procedures that their child will undergo, including an abortion.

The fundamental right of parents to be involved in decisions regarding their own children has been consistently recognized by the nation's highest court. This principle led the U.S. Supreme Court in 2000 to conclude in *Troxel v. Granville* that "it cannot now be doubted that the Due Process Clause of the Fourteenth Amendment protects the fundamental right of parents to make decisions concerning the care, custody, and control of their children."

The general public also shows overwhelming support for parental consent laws. A *Los Angeles Times* poll conducted in 2000 found that 82 percent of Americans agree that girls under the age of 18 should be required to obtain parental consent for an abortion. An earlier 1996 Gallop Survey found that 74 percent of Americans favored requiring parental consent for a minor's abortions.

The Effects of Parental Consent Laws

Several studies show that parental consent laws lead to a decrease in the abortion rate and teenage birth rate. A study that examined the impact of the Minnesota Parental Notification Law on abortion and birth found that the law led to a decrease of the teenage abortion rate by an average of 28 percent between the years of 1981–1986. The teenage birth rate also dropped an average of 10 percent during the same period.

Another study that examined the effects of parental involvement laws in Minnesota, Missouri, and Indiana found that in each state, the in-state abortion rate for minors fell with no evidence "that the laws [drove] up birth rates for minors." Researchers did speculate, however, that the decrease of in-state abortions could be due to minors traveling out of state for abortions.

A third study that examined the effect of state abortion restrictions on minors' demand for abortions stated that "results suggest that parental involvement laws decrease minors' demand for abortions by 13 to 25 percent and state restrictions on Medicaid funding of abortions decrease minors' demand for abortions by 9 to 17 percent."

After examining the flaws of all of the competing arguments, it becomes apparent that the debate over parental consent is not a debate over what is in the best interest of the child, but an extension of the abortion debate itself. Those who oppose parental notification laws are really not interested in the well-being of the children involved, but are fighting any limitation or regulation on the right to abortion. For these individuals, this is a political and ideological struggle that permeates any area that deals with reproduction. They see any regulation as a constraint on what they believe should be absolute sexual freedom. This is a goal they will pursue no matter what the cost to women, to children, or to society. . . .

Parental consent for abortion laws are a common sense approach to protecting young girls from making a potentially life changing decision without involving the people who most care for their well-being—their parents. It is important for any woman to enter a decision on this procedure with all the necessary information. And it is equally important for minor girls, who are often vulnerable and confused by their circumstances, to have the safeguard of counsel and support from their parents.

"The forced childbearing among teenagers that can result from parental consent and notice laws can have devastating effects on the health and life opportunities of young women and their children."

States Should Not Enforce Parental Consent Laws

NARAL Pro-Choice America

NARAL Pro-Choice America is a nonprofit reproductive rights and women's health advocacy group. In the following viewpoint the organization states its opposition to parental consent and notification laws, which require underage girls to notify their parents that they are getting an abortion or get written permission to have an abortion from one or both parents. Such laws can harm pregnant teens by delaying abortions, NARAL contends; the later an abortion is performed, they point out, the more dangerous it is to the woman. Moreover, many girls simply will not involve their parents and will obtain an illegal and unsafe abortion or commit suicide, the organization asserts.

As you read, consider the following questions:

1. According to the author, can the government mandate healthy family communication?
2. Have parental consent laws reduced abortion rates among pregnant teens, in the view of NARAL Pro-Choice America?
3. What percent of American women become pregnant before age 20, reports the author?

Loving parents should be involved when their daughters face crisis pregnancies. Every parent hopes that a child confronting a crisis will seek the advice and counsel of those who care for her most and know her best. In fact, even in the absence of laws mandating parental involvement, many young women do turn to their parents when they are considering an abortion. Unfortunately, some young women cannot involve their parents because they come from homes where physical violence or emotional abuse are prevalent or because their pregnancies are the result of incest. In other cases, young women may not realize how supportive their parents might be.

In some circumstances, teens facing a crisis pregnancy feel compelled to travel to another state where there is a less stringent parental involvement law or no such law at all, to avoid involving their parents and maintain their privacy. In the most dire circumstances, some pregnant young women who fear telling their parents may feel so desperate that they resort to illegal or self-induced abortions that may result in death. Yet, despite the severe consequences, 34 states currently enforce laws that require a minor to obtain the consent of, or notify, an adult—typically a parent—prior to an abortion. And ten other states have minors' access laws that are either enjoined or not enforced.

In an attempt to impose the most draconian state parental involvement laws on every other state in the country, Congress is considering legislation that would criminalize anyone other than a parent for accompanying a young woman across state lines for an abortion without the young woman first involving her parents or undergoing a judicial proceeding to waive her home state's parental involvement requirement. This legislation, deceptively called the "Child Custody Protection Act," [H.R. 476, the Child Custody Protection Act, was passed by the House of Representatives in 2002 but died later that year in the Senate Judiciary Committee], would threaten young women's health and deny them the support and guidance they need from responsible and caring adults.

Government cannot mandate healthy family communication. Laws requiring parental notice or consent actually harm the young women they purport to protect by increasing illegal and self-induced abortion, family violence, suicide, later abortions, and unwanted childbirth.

- In states that enforced no mandatory parental consent or notice requirement, 61 percent of parents knew of their daughters' pregnancy.
- The American Medical Association takes the position that: "Physicians should not feel or be compelled to require minors to involve their parents before deciding whether to undergo an abortion. . . . [M]inors should ultimately be allowed to decide whether parental involvement is appropriate."
- The American Academy of Pediatrics also opposes parental involvement laws: "Legislation mandating parental involvement does not achieve the intended benefit of promoting family communication but it does increase the risk of harm to the adolescent by delaying access to appropriate medical care. . . . [M]inors should not be compelled or required to involve their parents in their decisions to obtain abortions, although they should be encouraged to discuss their pregnancies with their parents and other responsible adults."
- Parental involvement laws appear to have had little effect on reducing abortion rates among teens.

Many Pregnant Teens Abused

Most young women find love, support and safety in their home. Many, however, justifiably fear that they would be physically or emotionally abused if forced to disclose their pregnancy. Often, young women who do not involve a parent come from families where government-mandated disclosure would have devastating effects.

- More than 3.2 million cases of child abuse were reported in 1999. Young women considering abortion are particularly vulnerable because family violence is often at its worst during a family member's pregnancy.
- Nearly half of pregnant teens who have a history of abuse report being assaulted during their pregnancy, most often by a family member. As the Supreme Court has recognized, "Mere notification of pregnancy is frequently a flashpoint for battering and violence within

the family. The number of battering incidents is high during the pregnancy and often the worst abuse can be associated with pregnancy."

- Among minors who did not tell a parent of their abortion, 30 percent had experienced violence in their family or feared violence or being forced to leave home.
- In Idaho, a 13-year-old student named Spring Adams was shot to death by her father after he learned she was to terminate a pregnancy caused by his acts of incest.

Parental consent and notice laws endanger young women's health by forcing some women—even those from healthy, loving families—to turn to illegal or self-induced abortion, to delay the procedure and increase the medical risk or to bear a child against their will.

- In Indiana, Rebecca Bell, a young woman who had a very close relationship with her parents, died from an illegal abortion that she sought because she did not want her parents to know about her pregnancy. Indiana law required parental consent before she could have a legal abortion.
- The American Medical Association has noted that "[b]ecause the need for privacy may be compelling, minors may be driven to desperate measures to maintain the confidentiality of their pregnancies. They may run away from home, obtain a 'back alley' abortion, or resort to self-induced abortion. The desire to maintain secrecy has been one of the leading reasons for illegal abortion deaths since . . . 1973."
- Recognizing that maintaining confidentiality is essential to minors' willingness to obtain necessary health care related to sexual activity, all 50 states and the District of Columbia authorize minors to consent to the diagnosis and treatment of sexually transmitted diseases without parental consent. In addition, the Supreme Court has recognized that confidential access to contraceptives is essential for minors to exercise their constitutional right to privacy, and federal law requires confidentiality for minors receiving family planning services through publicly funded programs, such as Title X and Medicaid.

- According to Leslie Tarr Laurie, president of Tapestry Health Systems, a Massachusetts-based health services provider: "Confidentiality is the cornerstone of our services. . . . We help teenagers avoid not only the costly and often tragic consequences of unintended pregnancy and childbearing, but also an early death from AIDS. The bottom line is, if we don't assure access to confidential health care, teenagers simply will stop seeking the care they desire and need."
- The American Medical Association concluded in a 1992 study that parental consent and notice laws "increase the gestational age at which the induced pregnancy termination occurs, thereby also increasing the risk associated with the procedure." Although a first or second trimester abortion is far safer than childbirth, the risk of complications significantly increases for each week that elapses after eight weeks.

Bypass Requirement Is Inadequate

In challenges to two different parental involvement laws, the Supreme Court has stated that a state statute requiring parental involvement must have some sort of bypass procedure, such as a judicial bypass, in order to be constitutional. No one person may have an absolute veto over a minor's decision to have an abortion. Thus, most states that require parental consent or notice provide—at least as a matter of law—a judicial bypass through which a young woman can seek a court order allowing an abortion without parental involvement. But bypass procedures are often an inadequate alternative for young women, especially when courts are either not equipped or resistant to granting judicial bypasses.

For adults, going to court for a judicial order is difficult. For young women without a lawyer, it is overwhelming and at times impossible. Some young women cannot maneuver the legal procedures required or cannot attend hearings scheduled during school hours. Others do not go or delay going because they fear that the proceedings are not confidential or that they will be recognized by people at the courthouse. Many experience fear and distress and do not want to reveal intimate details of their personal lives to strangers. The time

Consent Laws Risk Teen Pregnancies

Laws that require parental notification for teens to receive prescription contraception at family planning clinics could increase the risk of teen pregnancy, according to a study by Rachel Jones, Ph.D., and her colleagues.

"Family planning clinics need to be supported in the work that they are doing with teens," said Dr. Jones, senior research associate at the Alan Guttmacher Institute.

The study found that if a law required clinics to inform parents in writing when their teenagers got prescription birth control, 18% of teens would have sex using no contraceptive method or would rely on rhythm or withdrawal.

About 1% of teens surveyed said their only reaction to such a law would be to stop having sex, the study said.

Mary Ellen Schneider, *OB/GYN News*, February 15, 2005.

---

required to schedule the court proceeding may result in a delay of a week or more, thereby increasing the health risks of the abortion. And in many instances, courts are not equipped to handle bypass proceedings in accord with constitutional regulations. Worse yet, some young women who do manage to arrange a hearing face judges who are vehemently antichoice and who routinely deny petitions of minors who show that they are mature or that the bypass is in their best interest, despite rulings by the U.S. Supreme Court that the bypass must be granted in those circumstances.

- In denying the petition of one young woman, a Missouri judge stated: "Depending upon what ruling I make I hold in my hands the power to kill an unborn child. In our society it's a lot easier to kill an unborn child than the most vicious murderer. . . . I don't believe that this particular juvenile has sufficient intellectual capacity to make a determination that she is willing to kill her own child."

- A Toledo, Ohio judge denied a bypass for a 17-year-old woman, an "A" student who planned to attend college and who testified she was not financially or emotionally prepared for college and motherhood at the same time, stating that the girl had "not had enough hard knocks in her life."

- In Louisiana, a judge denied a 15-year-old a bypass petition after asking her a series of inappropriate questions, including what the minor would say to the fetus about her decision. Her request was granted only after a rehearing by six appellate court judges.
- A Pennsylvania study found that of the 60 judicial districts in the state, only eight were able to provide complete information about Pennsylvania's judicial bypass procedure. Some county courts referred minors to anti-choice crisis pregnancy centers that typically provide false and misleading information about abortion and pressure women to carry their pregnancies to term.
- The Alabama Supreme Court upheld a trial court's denial of a petition for a 17-year-old because the minor's testimony appeared "rehearsed" and she did not show "any emotion." The trial court refused to find that the minor was mature and well-informed enough to make her own decision or that an abortion was in her best interests—despite the fact that the 17-year-old high school senior had a 3.0 grade point average, had been accepted to college, had discussed her options with the father of the fetus, had spoken to a doctor, a counselor, her godmother, and her 20-year-old sister, was able to describe the abortion procedure, was informed about its risks, and had testified that her legal guardian had thrown a teenage relative out of the house when she became pregnant.

Notification Is a Risk to Teens

The forced childbearing among teenagers that can result from parental consent and notice laws can have devastating effects on the health and life opportunities of young women and their children.

- Approximately 40 percent of American women become pregnant before the age of 20.
- Teenage girls are more than 24 times more likely to die from childbirth than from first trimester legal abortions.
- Fewer than 60 percent of teen mothers graduate from high school by age 25—compared to 90 percent of those who postpone childbearing. Additionally, among African-

American and Hispanic teens, those who postpone child-bearing until age 20 are more likely to complete some college education.

- Twenty-five percent of teen mothers live below the federal poverty line. Nearly 80 percent of teen mothers eventually go on welfare. Teen mothers are also more likely to have lower family incomes in later life.
- Infants of teen mothers are one-third more likely to suffer from low birthweight (less than 5.5 pounds) than those born to older mothers. The children of teenage parents have an increased risk of abuse and neglect and are more likely to become teenage parents themselves, thus perpetuating the cycle of poverty.

Abortion among teenagers should be made less necessary, not more difficult and dangerous. A comprehensive approach to promoting adolescent reproductive health and reducing teen pregnancy will require an array of components, including:

- age-appropriate health and sex education with medically accurate information;
- access to confidential health services, including family planning and abortion;
- life options programs that offer teens practical life skills and the motivation to delay sexual activity; and
- programs for pregnant and parenting teens that teach parenting skills and help ensure that teens finish school.

Such an approach has never been implemented on a significant scale in the United States, and several studies of specific sexuality and AIDS education programs demonstrate positive outcomes such as increased knowledge, delay in onset of sex, reduction in the frequency of sex or increased contraceptive use. The wisest policy gives teenagers the tools they need to avoid pregnancy and forsakes misguided efforts to insert the government into delicate family situations.

> *"Contrary to what many experts suppose, young marriages undertaken to legitimate a pregnancy can be surprisingly durable."*

Unwed Teen Mothers Should Be Encouraged to Marry

Maggie Gallagher

In this viewpoint Maggie Gallagher argues that a teen girl should get married if she becomes pregnant. The author contends that teen marriages can be lasting, especially when family and friends support them. Gallagher calls for society to encourage, rather than discourage teens to marry when the girl gets pregnant, and she advocates for such programs as marriage education and marriage skills training. Gallagher is an affiliate scholar at the Institute for American Values, a nonprofit conservative organization.

As you read, consider the following questions:

1. How long, in the author's view, have Americans engaged in a campaign against teen marriage?
2. Are teen marriages made under duress always doomed to failure, according to Gallagher?
3. In the author's opinion, Congress should fund new programs to strengthen teen marriages in what type of communities?

Maggie Gallagher, "Is a Baby a Good Reason to Marry?" *American Experiment Quarterly*, vol. 4, Summer 2001, pp. 72–76. Copyright © 2001 by the Center for American Experiment. Reproduced by permission.

The relationship between marriage and babies has never been more tenuous in the minds of American young people. Evidence for this new disconnect abounds: in survey data, which tell us that while the overwhelming majority of girls who are high school seniors tell us that having a good marriage and family is "extremely important" to them personally, large majorities of single adult women are willing to consider single motherhood as an alternative. The *Time* magazine cover story "Who Needs a Husband?" (August 28, 2000) reported that 61 percent of unmarried women between the ages of eighteen and forty-nine in a *Time*/CNN poll said they would consider having a child without being married. The proportion of births to mothers who are not married continues to climb, reaching about a third in the latest census figures.

The 1990s witnessed an explosion in a strange new phenomenon: births to unmarried mothers who are nevertheless not yet single parents. About four in ten births outside of wedlock are now to cohabiting couples. In unprecedented numbers, young women today are having babies in fragile unions with men they live with and even say they love, but do not marry. Rates of legitimation of pregnancies have fallen dramatically. In the early 1970s, almost half of unmarried teens expecting their first baby married before the child's birth. By the early 1990s, less than one teen out of eight legitimated her pregnancy. Single pregnant women age eighteen and nineteen were three times more likely to choose unwed motherhood over marriage in the early 1990s compared to the early 1970s; even pregnant women in their early twenties were twice as likely to pick unwed motherhood over marriage. The big reason for our rising rates of unmarried childbearing is not that single women are so much more likely to get pregnant, but that single pregnant women are so much less likely to marry.

With their words and their actions, young women are telling us they no longer strongly connect marriage and childbearing. Marriage remains highly valued, but a baby is no longer seen as a good reason to get married. "I don't want him to feel he has to marry me," young mothers say in explaining why they aren't pressing for marriage. The expressive value of marriage as the ultimate symbol of true love is increasingly trumping the idea of marriage as a social institution—a practical context for the best baby-making and child rearing.

Reconnecting Babies and Marriage

What can we do to reconnect marriage and babies in the minds of young men and women?

First, we have to recognize that the decline in legitimation is no accident. For the past twenty years Americans have engaged in a moderately successful campaign against teen pregnancy, but for the past forty years Americans have engaged in an extremely successful campaign against early marriage, even marriage for the purpose of giving a baby a stable two-parent home. Young women who do not see a baby as a good reason to marry are in many ways conforming to rather than rebelling against the teachings of their elders. I put it this way in a 1999 Institute for American Values report, "The Age of Unwed Mothers: Is Teen Pregnancy the Problem?": "One infrequently acknowledged reason why fewer young mothers get married these days is that they are actively discouraged from doing so. As a society, our disapproval of early marriage has become ever sharper and more powerful, while our worries about unwed parenthood have become comparatively vague."

Here, for example, is the 1973 conclusion of two influential scholars: "Early marriages have not proved stable. . . . The rapid making and dissolution of a marriage with all its legal and financial complications may be more of a psychic trauma to the mother and her child than an attempt to raise a child within her parents' home or independently, or attempt to live unmarried in a temporary but loving relationship with a man." A year earlier, a Baptist minister proudly detailed his daughter's decision not to marry her child's father; she felt, "among other things, that to get married just for the child's sake was not adequate grounds for a healthy marriage." A 1992 RAND study noted that educators "applaud the decreasing incidence of marriage" among young mothers. And a 1996 high school health textbook warns that early marriage is "disastrous."

Warnings against shotgun marriages have survived despite a remarkable lack of research confirming these dire consequences in contemporary contexts and despite too an abundance of evidence detailing the very high risks for women and their children of the alternative: young unwed motherhood. Certainly it is better to delay both marriage and childbearing until the midtwenties. But is early marriage really a fate worse than unwed motherhood? Contrary to what many experts suppose, young marriages undertaken to legitimate a pregnancy can be surprisingly durable. In one study of pregnant single white women who married before giving birth to a child, 75 percent were still married ten years later.

Teens Are Being Misled

Sometimes, of course, young women choose as fathers for their children young men who are, frankly, not marriage material. But the conventional wisdom that marriages made under "duress" of childbearing are doomed to failure is simply not supported by the available evidence. Adults—clergy, educators, counselors—advise young pregnant women not to marry because they fear a shotgun marriage will only end in divorce and because they think young women are better off waiting to make better marriages in the future. They may be kidding themselves and misleading young women.

Young women who become unwed mothers permanently reduce their likelihood of making a lasting, stable marriage. One study found that young women who married to legitimate a pregnancy, for example, were at no higher risk of separation than similar young women with a postmarital conception, but that "having a premarital birth . . . significantly increases the probability of marital dissolution." And while young unwed mothers were no less likely than other women to say they expected to marry within the next five years, they were far less likely to achieve that aspiration (45 percent of childless women who expected to marry did so within five years, compared to 28 percent of unwed mothers). As these researchers concluded, "It seems women generally are not having children nonmaritally as a response to poor marriage prospects. Rather, having a child outside of marriage appears to derail young women's existing plans."

The first step in reconnecting marriage and babies in the minds of the younger generations is for parents, family scholars, social workers, marriage counselors, clergy, and educators to reevaluate their own prejudices against marriage undertaken to legitimate a pregnancy. Is a baby a good reason to get married? At least a good reason to marry a decent guy you love and are living with? Until adults in the community can unambiguously say yes to young men and women, we cannot expect young people to stumble upon this truth on their own. Marriage means many things to many people, but a man and a woman who marry in order to work together to make a happy home for their child should not be stigmatized as "having" to marry, or as "settling" for an inferior product—they are expressing a loving marriage ideal of the highest order, worth honoring and striving for. Americans will be more comfortable promoting marriage to young parents when we recognize that this is essentially an affirmative and not a punitive strategy: marriage is not a punishment for sexual sin, but simply the best outcome for mothers, fathers, and children alike.

Right now there is a dense network of formal and informal government, community, and faith-based programs designed to help young unwed mothers overcome the obstacles posed by having children outside of marriage, in terms of a young woman's health, education, and job prospects. There is no similar network of community and church-based organizations dedicated to helping young parents translate their feelings of love for each other and their child into stable, healthy marriages.

Changing this state of affairs would be the first step toward reversing the growing disconnect between marriage and childbearing. Here are three ideas for fostering such programs and such community change.

First, the National Institutes of Health, joined by private philanthropies, should sponsor rigorous scientific research on the benefits and risks of marriage and adoption and unwed motherhood for pregnant women under the age of twenty-five. Better and more definitive research would help overturn the existing social prejudices among influential elites against legitimating pregnancies.

Examining Attitudes About Teens and Marriage

"Teen pregnancy prevention programs should teach young people to be married before they have a child."

	ADULTS	TEENS
AGREE STRONGLY	73%	63%
AGREE SOMEWHAT	13%	21%
DISAGREE SOMEWHAT	7%	10%
DISAGREE STRONGLY	6%	6%

ADULTS				TEENS
86%	AGREE NET	84%		
	13%	DISAGREE NET	16%	

"With One Voice 2002: America's Adults and Teens Sound Off About Teen Pregnancy," An Annual National Survey, December 2002. The National Campaign to Prevent Teen Pregnancy.

Second, all government-funded teen pregnancy programs should be required to teach teenagers that, ideally, they should wait until marriage before they bring a child into the world. Why should you wait to have a baby? What are you waiting for? Right now, the answers most adults give youngsters suggest that if you have a high school diploma, or turn twenty-one, our warnings against "teen" pregnancy do not apply. Sound educational principles, if nothing else, require that we inform children of what the weight of social science evidence teaches: all things being equal, children do better when they are raised by their own two married parents. And as Professor Linda J. Waite and I point out in our new book, *The Case for Marriage: Why Married People Are Happier, Healthier, and Better-Off Financially*, marriage provides important protections for adults and communities as well.

But such information is likely to be diluted and relatively ineffective if it is delivered only through the existing program network, often administered by program elites who (quite wrongly, in my view) see marriage as an inherently judgmental and divisive goal. (Curious that the same people who have no trouble telling a poor young mother she can dream big in terms of her career—be a doctor or a lawyer or any other noble but unlikely ambition—view encouraging her to reach for a happy marriage as not only moralistic but also unrealistic.)

Therefore, . . . Congress should create a new dedicated

funding stream for programs aimed at strengthening marriage in low-income communities, with the triple goal of avoiding divorce among low-income at-risk married couples, supporting young pregnant women who choose to marry, and encouraging young cohabiting couples to make healthy marriages. Promising strategies for achieving these programmatic goals include new teen pregnancy programs aimed at delaying childbirth until marriage; divorce mediation aimed at encouraging reconciliations as well as reducing acrimony and litigation; vouchers or tax credit for marriage education programs; job training and other income assistance directed at low-income husbands and cohabiting couples who marry; marriage skills training and other assistance for unemployed fathers.

At this point, encouraging a variety of programmatic options delivered by professionals enthusiastically dedicated to helping marriages take place and succeed is the most important step. Funds for rigorous scientific research evaluating such programs should be appropriated at the same time. Teen pregnancy programs wasted about fifteen years throwing money at the problem based on theoretical approaches before sound evaluation research finally pointed communities toward the kinds of practical programs that actually work to help reduce teen pregnancy rates. Those of us who care about supporting and promoting marriage should avoid the similar fantasy that good intentions matter more than good results.

Can we reconnect marriage and childbearing? Can we reduce unmarried childbearing and help more cohabiting couples move toward marriage and help more at-risk marriages succeed? I believe so, especially if we move to a new model of positive and not punitive strategies to strengthen marriage. When adults came together to give teens the message that it is better to wait to have babies, the result was a dramatic and otherwise inexplicable reduction in teen births. True, out-of-wedlock births to women in their early twenties continued to rise, but that is more our fault than theirs. Imagine what might happen if responsible adults were able to tell the next generation of young men and women what exactly they were waiting for.

"Some policymakers and others may assume that any teen mother . . . would be better off married. There is good reason to believe, however, that such a blanket assumption may be wrong."

Unwed Teen Mothers Should Not Be Encouraged to Marry

Naomi Seiler

Naomi Seiler is a Greenwall Fellow in bioethics and health policy at the Johns Hopkins School of Public Health. In the following viewpoint she argues that the government should not encourage unwed teen mothers to marry because these marriages are often unstable. Such marriages also involve higher rates of abuse, she claims. Instead, Seiler says, the government and society should concentrate on pregnancy prevention programs that research shows are successful in reducing teen births.

As you read, consider the following questions:
1. What were the median ages of first marriages for women in 1890 and 1998, according to Seiler?
2. One-half of teen marriages, the author writes, will end in divorce within how many years?
3. In Seiler's view what age group of females experiences the highest rates of domestic violence?

Naomi Seiler, *Is Teen Marriage a Solution?* Washington, DC: Center for Law and Social Policy, 2002. Copyright © 2002 by the Center for Law and Social Policy. Reproduced by permission.

M ost Americans are probably not aware that the 1996 legislation that changed America's welfare system also included several provisions related to marriage and family formation. In fact, three of the four purposes of the law encourage states to promote marriage, "the formation and maintenance of two-parent families," and the reduction of out-of-wedlock pregnancies. The law also provides bonuses to states that decrease the proportion of their births that are "out-of-wedlock" and includes federal funds for programs for teens that promote the practice of abstinence-unless-married. And these provisions are not always limited to welfare families.

The promotion and maintenance of marriage has become a major focus in the debate over reauthorization of the welfare program, Temporary Assistance for Needy Families (TANF), scheduled for fall 2002. In one well-publicized proposal, Robert Rector of the Heritage Foundation suggests earmarking 10 percent of all TANF funds for marriage education and other related activities. Targeting teens more directly, he has also proposed a demonstration that provides up to $10,000 to young, "at-risk girls" under age 18 who do not bear children before age 21 and avoid a premarital birth. Charles Murray of the American Enterprise Institute has suggested a one-state experiment in which all means-tested benefits are cut off for unwed mothers under age 18. In addition, federally-funded abstinence-unless-married education, which contends that sex outside of marriage is unhealthy, may have the unintended consequence of encouraging teens to marry before they are ready.

Because many of these policy proposals could have the effect—intended or unintended—of encouraging teens to marry, this paper discusses the potential implications of teen marriage. Should teenage girls who become pregnant be encouraged to marry? What might the effects be on a young woman, on her child, or on the child's father? What do we know about how teen marriage patterns vary with age, race, and other factors? Because policy concerns center on teens who become pregnant, most of the studies cited here focus on marriages related to pregnancy.

Marriage is certainly one (formerly common) route to reduce out-of-wedlock births by those teens who become pregnant; however, there is reason to be concerned that such marriages are often unstable. In contrast, preventing teen pregnancy in the first place carries with it none of these concerns. A focus on teen pregnancy prevention is particularly appropriate in any effort to address out-of-wedlock births because 80 percent of teen births are out-of-wedlock and 50 percent of non-marital *first* births are to teens (and it is these first births that are driving the increase in out-of-wedlock childbearing). Since many teenagers want to avoid unintended pregnancy, it makes sense to help them achieve this personal and public goal. Focusing on the responsibilities of parenting, the potential value of two parents to children, and the virtue in delaying parenting until one is ready could all be part of a strategy to prevent teen pregnancy. And researchers have now defined what works: a relatively new body of rigorous research demonstrates that a variety of teen pregnancy prevention programs can succeed in reducing teen births.

Based on our review of the data, the Center for Law and Social Policy (CLASP) believes the government should temper any enthusiasm for marriage with a respect for its complex human nature and a recognition of how little we know about what works to promote marriage; policies that directly or indirectly encourage teen marriage raise additional concerns. While CLASP supports efforts to help couples voluntarily strengthen their relationships and marriages and believes some teen marriages can prove beneficial, it would be unfortunate if the result of government policy were to foster too-early teen marriages.

Some policymakers and others may assume that any teen mother with a baby would be better off married. There is good reason to believe, however, that such a blanket assumption may be wrong. Marriage of the very young mother may merely replace one public concern, "premature parenting," with another: "premature marriage."

Teen Marriage Trends Have Changed Since 1960s

The first step in assessing policy proposals that might encourage teen marriage is to review what we know about the past and current trends in marriage among teens and in nonmarital teen fertility. Much has changed in these areas in the last 40 years.

The "delaying" of first marriage today is actually part of a larger history of falling and rising median ages at first marriage. Marital age for both men and women has been affected by a complex interaction of historical events, social changes, and educational and professional expectations. Median ages of first marriage today are higher than they were in the 1950s and 1960s, a time when marital ages were unusually low. In 1998, men's median age at first marriage was 26.7, only six months older than it was in 1890. Women's numbers have increased more; their median age at first marriage was 22 in 1890, dipped down to 20.1 in 1956, and by 1998 reached 25.

Rates of teen marriage today vary by sex and race. In March of 1998, approximately 1 percent of all 15- to 17-year-olds had ever been married. Older teens were more likely to have been married; 6.5 percent of white women and 13.4 percent of Hispanic women aged 18–19 had ever been married. In total, approximately 450,000 15- to 19-year-olds had ever been married in March 1998.

Different regions of the country have very different rates of teen marriage. In March of 1998, teens in the South and West were more likely to have been married than those in the Northeast and Midwest, with the gap growing by age 18–19. Only 1.7 percent of 18- to 19-year-olds in the Northeast had ever been married, compared to 6.1 percent in the South.

Unwed Teen Fertility Rates Are High

Teens represent a diminishing share of women who give birth outside of marriage . . . In 1970, one-half of births to unmarried women were among teenagers; in 1999, 29 percent were to teens. The percentage of births to unmarried women of all ages has increased from 4 percent in 1950 to 33 percent in 1999. This is due to an increase in the proportion of unmarried women among those of reproductive age, a decrease in fertility rates of married women, and an increase in fertility rates of unmarried women.

. . . but teen nonmarital fertility rates remain high. The

birth rate for unmarried teens age 15–19 rose from 12.6 per 1000 in 1950 to 46.4 per 1000 in 1994, dropping to 40.4 by 1999. Together, nonmarital births to teenagers and to adult women whose first births occurred as teens account for over one-half of nonmarital births.

The fathers of babies born to teen girls vary in age, but relationships between teen girls and older partners are associated with a disproportionate number of pregnancies. In 1994, among sexually experienced women under 18, 65 percent of those with partners six or more years older became pregnant, compared to 18 percent of those whose partners were no more than two years older. The same pattern, in which the pregnancy rate is higher the older the partner, held true for all girls under 20 who were married at conception. Further, married women under 20 were more than twice as likely to become pregnant than those not married. In addition, among sexually active girls aged 15–17, men who were six or more years older represented 6.7 percent of partners; however, they caused a disproportionate percent of pregnancies (19.2 percent), unintended births (22.2 percent), and intended births (27.9 percent).

"Shotgun" Teen Marriages Have Declined

Steep declines in the proportion of pregnant teens who enter "shotgun" marriages have contributed to the high rates of nonmarital pregnancies among teens. Though older teens are more likely to marry between the conception and birth of their child than younger teens, rates of "shotgun" marriage have declined greatly for all teens as well as for older women. From the first half of the 1960s to the first half of the 1990s, the marriage rate for pregnant teens fell from 69.4 percent to 19.3 percent for whites, and from 36.0 percent to 6.7 percent for blacks.

Of first births to 15- to 19-year-olds, a higher proportion are conceived premaritally today than 70 years ago. In the early 1930s, less than one-third of first births to teens aged 15–19 were conceived premaritally. By the early 1990s, this proportion had risen to over 80 percent.

The traits of male partners also affect whether a pregnancy leads to marriage before birth (although data specific to teens are not available). Different factors affect the likelihood of black and white males marrying to resolve a nonmarital pregnancy. In one study, among white males, employment led to slightly increased rates of marriage, while for black males, employment status did not affect the rate. However, a smaller study focusing on low-income men showed that employed fathers are twice as likely to marry as unemployed fathers. Before 1980, educational background did not affect the likelihood of white males' marrying between conception and birth, but from 1980–1990 being enrolled in or completing high school was positively associated with the likelihood of marriage for this group. Black males were more likely to marry between conception and birth if they lived in the South, and increased age led to a higher likelihood of marriage for black but not white men. Males who are five or more years older than their partners account for a small portion (8 percent) of all teen births under age eighteen. This age difference would subject the males to statutory rape prosecution in many states, even if the sex were consensual. However, some states have allowed the males to marry their teen partners to avoid prosecution.

All Nonmarital Births, 1992–1995

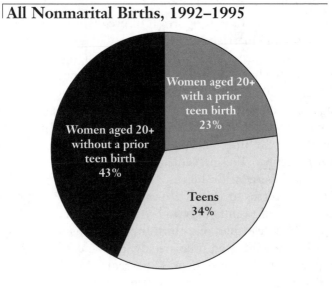

Women aged 20+ with a prior teen birth
23%

Women aged 20+ without a prior teen birth
43%

Teens
34%

Child Trends, 2001.

Teen Marriages Are the Most Unstable

What do we know about the long-term stability of teen marriages? How does getting married as a teen affect the economic prospects of the family? What other effects does teen marriage have on the health and well-being of teens? Current research offers some preliminary (and not always consistent) answers to these questions and also suggests areas for which we need to find out more.

Early marriages are the most unstable. While divorce and separation rates are high in the U.S. overall, rates are particularly high for teen marriages. For instance, about one-half of teen marriages (among women aged 18–19) will end in divorce within fifteen years, compared to about one-third of marriages for women over twenty. In 1995, women who had married as teens were far more likely to have undergone a marital dissolution than those who married even just a few years later. While the effect is particularly dramatic for women who married before age 18, even older teens who marry experience divorce and separation at higher rates than those who wait until they are out of their teens.

Unwed mothers have relatively low future prospects of marriage. While data specific to teen mothers have not been analyzed, women who bear a child without marrying have a 40 percent lower likelihood of ever marrying than those who don't, controlling for age, race, and socioeconomic status. Therefore, teen mothers who do not marry once pregnant may have diminished prospects of ever marrying.

Marrying can improve an unwed mother's economic outlook (although an analysis exclusively on teens is not available). In 1995, previously unwed mothers who were currently married had a poverty rate less than one-third that of their never-married counterparts.

The instability of an early marriage can jeopardize its potential for economic good. For unwed mothers of all ages, marrying and then divorcing correlates with higher risks of poverty than never marrying. While data have not been analyzed separately for teen marriages, teenage girls who have a nonmarital birth and then marry and divorce may also be worse off economically than those who do not marry.

When the fathers of teens' babies are teens themselves,

they may have less financial resources to contribute. Teen males who become fathers earn less in early adulthood than males who delay parenting until after age 20. Teen fathers earn more than those who delay fatherhood from age 17–22, but after age 22 their incomes steadily lag behind males who were not teen fathers. This gap may be linked to lower educational attainment among teenage fathers, though it is difficult to separate cause from effect.

Marrying before the birth of a child may lead to greater paternal support, even if the marriage doesn't last. If couples marry, the male partner is likely to be a residential parent and have greater access to the child. Even if the couple eventually divorces, this early contact may lead to greater levels of financial support from the father.

The Health of Teen Mothers

Young mothers who marry are more likely to have a rapid second birth. According to a national longitudinal study, teen mothers are more likely to have a rapid second birth if they marry. Results from a national program for teenage mothers showed a similar correlation between living with a partner or husband and the likelihood of a subsequent pregnancy. Closely-spaced second births are linked to worse economic and educational outcomes for both the young mother and her child.

Teen marriage may lead to decreased educational attainment for girls. If marriage is associated with a higher chance of a closely-spaced second birth and if teen mothers with two or more children face a greater likelihood of lower educational attainment, then early marriage may intensify the educational harms of early childbearing. A study based on the National Survey of Family Growth and the National Longitudinal Youth Survey revealed trends that support this idea. Girls who married between conception and birth were less likely to return to school than those who didn't marry. Six months after birth, the correlation was seen for both races but was statistically significant only among black teens, who returned to school within six months at a rate of 56.4 percent if unmarried but only at a rate of 14.9 percent if they married between conception and birth. The same correlation was seen in rates of ever returning to school after childbirth, and was statistically significant for both whites and blacks.

Young relationships often involve high levels of violence. There are no data available on the rates of violence experienced by young women who are married versus those who are not, but any policy or demonstration program encouraging teens to marry should recognize that young relationships often involve relatively high rates of violence. The U.S. Department of Justice reports that women aged 16–24 are the age group experiencing the highest rates of violent victimization by intimates, including murder, rape, sexual assault, robbery, and aggravated and simple assaults. Other research indicates that, for some teen mothers, an antecedent of their sexual activity and teen pregnancy is the experience of abuse in childhood. At the same time, there is anecdotal evidence from older research that some teens marry to escape abusive or otherwise problematic homes.

Reasons to Question Teen Marriages

It is likely that, as with all women, teens experience some current economic benefit from being married. However, there are a number of important reasons to question an assumption that a teen mother who is not inclined to marry would be better off married. Notably, high rates of dissolution of teen marriages may make marriage a riskier bet for teen women's long-term economic security than it is for older women. Since married teens are more likely to have a rapid repeat birth and this can affect school completion, marriage may hamper future economic stability. The high rates of abuse by intimates that young women experience suggest yet another reason to be cautious.

For those teens who do marry, we urge policymakers to provide support services to help them build strong relationships. However, the instability of teen marriage and the risks it can pose should give pause to any policymaker who is eager to encourage pregnant adolescents to walk down the aisle.

Periodical Bibliography

The following articles have been selected to supplement the diverse views presented in this chapter.

Kevin Brady and Jan Schakowsky	"Do Parents Always Have a Right to Know When Their Teen Is Seeking Birth Control?" *Insight on the News*, October 29, 2002.
Margaret Bernstein and Robert L. Smith	"The Price of Poverty: Culture of Marriage Disappearing," *Plain Dealer*, January 2, 2005.
Cynthia Dailard	"Statutory Rape Reporting and Family Planning Programs: Moving Beyond Conflict," *Guttmacher Report on Public Policy*, June 2004.
Sally Feldman	"Why I'm Glad My Daughter Had Underage Sex; Amid the Clamors for Censorship, Celibacy, and an End to Teenagers' Rights to Confidentiality, British Journalist Sally Feldman Fulminates Against Her Country's Misguided Moral Crusaders," *Humanist*, November/December 2004.
Joe Feuerherd	"Bush's Antipoverty Weapon: Nonprofits Say 'I Do' to Funds for Strengthening Marriages; Critics See Better Use for Federal Money," *National Catholic Reporter*, November 28, 2003.
D. Hollander	"Many Parents of Teenagers Think Parental Involvement Laws Will Increase Risks," *Perspectives on Sexual Reproductive Health*, June 2005.
Kate O'Beirne	"Altered States: Bush Tries to Promote Marriage Through Welfare Reform," *National Review*, May 6, 2002.
Suzanne Ryan et al.	"The Relationship Between Teenage Motherhood and Marriage," *Science Says*, September 2004.
Cody Sain	"Parental Notification Laws Must Be Made Consistent," *Battalion*, February 23, 2005.
Miranda Sawyer	"Sex Is Not Just for Grown-Ups," *Observer*, November 2, 2003.
Mary Ellen Schneider	"Study: Parental Notification Laws May Lead to More Teen Pregnancies," *OB/GYN News*, February 15, 2005.
Naomi Seiler	"Is Teen Marriage a Solution?" April 2002. www.clasp.org.
Paola Totaro	"Age of Consent for Gay Males Will Be Cut to 16, Says Labor," *Sydney Morning Herald*, May 7, 2003.

CHAPTER 4

What Should Teens Be Taught About Sex?

Chapter Preface

"Friends with benefits." The phrase sounds innocent enough but for many teens in America "benefits" mean oral sex. With parents, schools, government, and American society placing a strong emphasis on adolescents refraining from sex until marriage, some adolescents have found a way around the prohibition: They have redefined what constitutes sex. A handful of studies since the late 1990s show an increasing number of teens—40 percent in a survey of teen readers by *Seventeen* magazine—do not consider oral sex as sex. A report issued in September 2005 by the Centers for Disease Control and Prevention shows one in four teen virgins has had oral sex. One study of ninth graders by the University of California at San Francisco (UCSF) found that teens are increasingly more likely to try oral sex. These and other reports suggest that teens believe oral sex is less risky to their emotional and physical health than is vaginal or anal sex.

The trend toward more oral sex among teens has changed the debate on what teens should be taught about sex. Unless the dangers associated with oral sex are discussed with teens, many experts contend, youths are at risk of sexually transmitted diseases (STDs). Some teens simply see oral sex as a form of kissing and are unaware that STDs can be transmitted through oral sex even if there is no ejaculation. Primary among these diseases are the human papillomavirus (HPV), herpes I and II, gonorrhea, and syphilis. HIV and chlamydia can also be transmitted through oral sex, although to a lesser degree. Condoms and dental dams reduce the risk of acquiring STDs through oral sex. "Adults should discuss more than one type of sexual practice when they counsel teens," said Bonnie Halpern-Felsher, associate professor of adolescent medicine at UCSF.

> The fact that young adolescents around age 14 are having or considering oral sex and consider it safer and more acceptable than vaginal sex is important information for parents, health care providers, and others who work with youth. When we counsel adolescents about the risks and benefits associated with sex, we need to understand how they perceive it among themselves.

A growing body of information exists on why teens are engaging in more oral sex. In a 2002 episode of the *Oprah Winfrey Show*, Winfrey and Dr. Phil discussed this new and casual view of oral sex with a group of teens. The youths described having oral sex with people they were not dating, simply because they wanted to. The teens said that adults who thought of oral sex as intimate were old-fashioned. A northern California magazine, *Metroactive*, interviewed twenty-five Sonoma, California, teens and found oral sex to be common. Fourteen-year-old Ashley said she first performed oral sex on a boy when she was eleven. She said in most cases girls give oral sex to boys because they feel they have to in order to keep their boyfriends. "In today's girl-power world, some girls view oral sex as a means to assert control over when and how they are sexual," said the article's author, Joy Lanzendorfer. "Some may even use oral sex as a way to maintain their virginity while still pleasing their boyfriends."

Authors in the following chapter examine what teens should be taught about sex. As more and more teens engage in oral sex, pressure is building to include information about oral sex in all sexual education programs.

"The findings presented in this paper strongly suggest that virginity pledge and similar abstinence education programs have the potential to substantially reduce teen sexual activity, teen pregnancy, and out-of-wedlock childbearing."

Abstinence-Only Programs Work

Robert Rector, Kirk A. Johnson, and Jennifer A. Marshall

Robert Rector is senior research fellow in domestic policy, Kirk A. Johnson is senior policy analyst in the Center for Data Analysis, and Jennifer A. Marshall is director of domestic policy studies, all at the Heritage Foundation, a conservative think tank. In this viewpoint the authors use research data from several previous studies to conclude that a commitment to abstinence has an overall positive effect on teens' lives. The authors contend that abstinence programs such as virginity pledges delay teens' first sexual encounters and result in fewer unwanted teen pregnancies.

As you read, consider the following questions:

1. As reported by Rector, Johnson, and Marshall, what percent of teens that have never taken a virginity pledge have had sex before age 18?
2. To practice abstinence, teens must resist pressure from what two groups, as stated by the authors?
3. What negative risky behaviors are associated with taking a virginity pledge, according to the authors?

Adolescents who take a virginity pledge have substantially lower levels of sexual activity and better life outcomes when compared with similar adolescents who do not make such a pledge, according to recently released data from the National Longitudinal Study of Adolescent Health (Add Health survey). Specifically, adolescents who make a virginity pledge:

- Are less likely to experience teen pregnancy;
- Are less likely to be sexually active while in high school and as young adults;
- Are less likely to give birth as teens or young adults;
- Are less likely to give birth out of wedlock;
- Are less likely to engage in risky unprotected sex; and
- Will have fewer sexual partners.

In addition, making a virginity pledge is not associated with any long-term negative outcomes. For example, teen pledgers who do become sexually active are not less likely to use contraception.

Data from the National Longitudinal Study of Adolescent Health, which is funded by more than 17 federal agencies, show that the behavior of adolescents who have made a virginity pledge is significantly different from that of peers who have not made a pledge. Teenage girls who have taken a virginity pledge are one-third less likely to experience a pregnancy before age 18. Girls who are strong pledgers (defined as those who are consistent in reporting a virginity pledge in the succeeding waves of the Add Health survey) are more than 50 percent less likely to have a teen pregnancy than are non-pledgers.

Teens who make a virginity pledge are far less likely to be sexually active during high school years. Nearly two-thirds of teens who have never taken a pledge are sexually active before age 18; by contrast, only 30 percent of teens who consistently report having made a pledge become sexually active before age 18.

Teens who have made a virginity pledge have almost half as many lifetime sexual partners as non-pledgers have. By the time they reach their early twenties, non-pledgers have had, on average, six different sex partners; pledgers, by contrast, have had three.

Girls and Virginity Pledges

Girls who have taken a virginity pledge are one-third less likely to have an out-of-wedlock birth when compared with those who have never taken a pledge. Girls who are strong pledgers (those who are consistent in reporting a virginity pledge in the succeeding waves of the Add Health survey) are half as likely to have an out-of-wedlock birth as are non-pledgers.

Girls who make a virginity pledge also have fewer births overall (both marital and nonmarital) as teens and young adults than do girls who do not make pledges. By the time they reach their early twenties, some 27.2 percent of the young women who have never made a virginity pledge have given birth. By contrast, the overall birth rate of peers who have made a pledge is nearly one-third lower, at 19.8 percent.

Because they are less likely to be sexually active, pledging teens are less likely to engage in unprotected sex, especially unprotected nonmarital sex. For example, 28 percent of non-pledging youth reported engaging in unprotected non-marital sex during the past year, compared with 22 percent of all pledgers and 17 percent of strong pledgers.

Teen Pregnancy (Females Only)

	Non-Pledgers	All Pledgers	Strong Pledgers	Weak Pledgers
Percent with Pregnancy Before 18th Birthday	9.70%	6.50%	4.30%	8.10%

National Longitudinal Study of Adolescent Health, 2004.

One possible explanation for the differences in behavior between pledgers and non-pledgers is that the two groups differ in important social background factors such as socio-economic status, race, religiosity, and school performance. It is possible that these background factors—rather than the pledge *per se*—account for the differences in sexual behavior and birth rates.

To investigate this possibility, the authors performed multivariate regression analyses that compared individuals who were identical in relevant background factors. These analyses show that, although the magnitude of the differences was reduced somewhat, differences in the behavior of pledging and non-pledging teens persisted even when background factors such as socioeconomic status, race, religiosity, and other relevant variables were held constant.

Overall, making a virginity pledge is strongly associated with a wide array of positive behaviors and outcomes while having no negative effects. The findings presented in this paper strongly suggest that virginity pledge and similar abstinence education programs have the potential to substantially reduce teen sexual activity, teen pregnancy, and out-of-wedlock childbearing. . . .

Virginity Pledgers Are Less Likely to Experience Teen Pregnancy

The Add Health survey data show that girls who have made a virginity pledge are substantially less likely to experience teen pregnancy (to become pregnant before their 18th birthday) when compared with girls who have not made a pledge. . . . Some 6.5 percent of girls who had made a pledge became pregnant before age 18. The figure for girls who had not made a pledge was about 50 percent higher, at 9.7 percent. Among girls who were strong pledgers, the pregnancy rate was lower still: 4.3 percent became pregnant before their 18th birthday—less than half the number among non-pledgers.

The Add Health survey data show that teens who have made a virginity pledge are likely to delay substantially the onset of sexual activity, compared with those who have not made a pledge. . . . Among non-pledgers, the median age for beginning sexual intercourse was 16 years and 11 months. By contrast, the median age for the onset of sexual activity among all pledging teens was 21 months later, at 18 years and 8 months. The delay in the onset of sexual activity was even more pronounced in the strong pledger group; the median age of initial sexual activity among these teens was 19 years and 9 months, or nearly three years later than the non-pledgers. . . .

Positive Effects of Abstinence

The Add Health survey provides a wealth of important data about the sexual behavior of teens and young adults. These data reveal two clear facts about teens and virginity pledges.

- *Fact #1:* Teens who make virginity pledges have far better life outcomes and are far less likely to engage in risky sexual behavior when compared with teens who do not pledge. In general, teens who make virginity pledges are much less likely to become sexually active while in high school, to experience a teen pregnancy, and to have children out of wedlock. Compared with non-pledgers, teens who pledge have substantially fewer sex partners and are less likely to engage in unprotected sexual activity.
- *Fact #2:* The behavioral differences between pledging and non-pledging teens cannot be explained by differences in social background characteristics such as race, family income, and religiosity. Holding social factors constant, taking a virginity pledge is independently correlated with a broad array of positive behaviors and life outcomes.

Overall, the evidence concerning the positive effects of virginity pledges is extremely strong. Nevertheless, skeptics might argue that the simple fact that teens who make virginity pledges have substantially improved behaviors does not prove that virginity pledge programs themselves have a positive impact on behavior. It is conceivable that participating in a virginity pledge program and taking a pledge merely reinforce pro-abstinence decisions that the teen would have made without the program or pledge. From this perspective, virginity pledge programs may be a redundant "fifth wheel" that has no effect, rather than an operative factor leading to less risk-related behavior.

Given the limitations of the Add Health data, it is impossible to fully disprove this type of skepticism. Nonetheless, such an argument goes against common sense. Teens do not make decisions about sexual values in a vacuum. A decision to abstain and delay sexual activity does not emerge in a teen's mind [from nowhere] but rather will reflect the sexual values and messages that society communicates to the adolescent.

Teens Must Resist Social Pressures

Regrettably, teens today live in a sex-saturated popular culture that celebrates casual sex at an early age. To practice abstinence, teens must resist pressure from peers and the media, in addition to controlling physical desire. It seems implausible to expect teens to abstain from sexual activity in the absence of social institutions (such as virginity pledge programs) that teach strong abstinence values. Similarly, it seems implausible that programs that teach clear abstinence values will have no influence on behavior, even among teens who embrace those values.

Since decisions to practice abstinence do not emerge in a vacuum, it seems very likely that the messages in virginity pledge programs contribute to positive behavior among youth. Participation in virginity pledge programs encourages youth to make pro-abstinence choices, and publicly taking an abstinence pledge reinforces teens' commitment to this decision and helps them to stick with the abstinence lifestyle.

The bottom line is simple: Teens who participate in virginity pledge programs and respond affirmatively to the messages in the program are far less likely to engage in risky behaviors and will have far better life outcomes than those who do not. Consequently, it would be best to expose teens to more, rather than fewer, pro-abstinence messages.

Teens who make virginity pledges promise to remain virgins until marriage. While many pledgers fail to meet that goal, as a group, teens who make virginity pledges have substantially improved behaviors compared with non-pledgers. Teens who make pledges have better life outcomes and are far less likely to engage in risky behaviors. As a whole, teen pledgers will have fewer sexual partners and are less likely to become sexually active in high school. Pledgers are less likely to experience teen pregnancy, less likely to give birth out of wedlock, and less likely to engage in unprotected sexual activity. These positive outcomes are linked to the act of making the pledge itself and are not the result of social background factors.

In addition, there are no negative risky behaviors associated with taking a virginity pledge. For example, pledgers who become sexually active are not less likely to use contraception. Thus, teens have everything to gain and nothing to lose from virginity pledge programs. Such programs appear to have a strong and significant effect in encouraging positive and constructive behavior among youth.

Today's teens, however, live in sex-saturated culture, and positive influences that counteract the tide of permissiveness are scattered and weak. Relatively few youth are exposed to the affirmative messages coming from virginity pledge programs and similar abstinence education programs. Sadly, despite polls showing that nearly all parents want youth to be taught a strong abstinence message, abstinence education is rare in American schools. While it is true that, bowing to popular pressure, most current sex education curricula claim that they promote abstinence, in reality, these programs pay little more than lip service to the topic. Most, in fact, are permeated by anti-abstinence themes.

Still, parents continue to support abstinence values and to realize that good abstinence education programs can positively affect youth behavior. It is regrettable that most schools fail to meet either parents' expectations or students' needs.

"Sexually active teens cannot protect themselves from disease and pregnancy without full and accurate information about the transmission of [sexually transmitted infections], their treatment, and the effectiveness of contraception."

Abstinence-Only Programs Do Not Work

American Civil Liberties Union

The American Civil Liberties Union (ACLU) argues in the following viewpoint that abstinence-only sex education programs in high schools are ineffective. The ACLU states that these programs do not help teens delay having sex until marriage, nor do they reduce teen pregnancies or sexually transmitted diseases. Abstinence-only education fails because it deters teens from using condoms and other contraceptives when having sex, according to the ACLU. The ACLU is a civil rights and individual liberties advocacy group.

As you read, consider the following questions:

1. Do comprehensive sex education programs that promote safer sex increase the number of teens having sex, according to the ACLU?
2. How do abstinence-only programs, in the view of the ACLU, affect gay and lesbian teens?
3. In the ACLU's opinion, an overwhelming majority of parents want sex education programs to include coverage of what topics?

Despite statistics that demonstrate a high level of sexual activity and risk-taking behavior among U.S. teens, Congress has allocated well over half a billion dollars since 1997 for educational programs that focus exclusively on abstinence and censor other information that can help young people make responsible, healthy, and safe decisions about sexual activity. There is no conclusive evidence to date that these programs reduce the rate of unintended pregnancy or sexually transmitted infections (STIs), and there is some evidence that shows that they deter sexually active teens from using condoms and other contraceptives. Moreover, research indicates that many of these programs do not help teens delay having sex. Nevertheless, in recent years federal lawmakers have steadily increased federal funding to more than $165 million annually. In contrast, no federal funds are dedicated to supporting programs that teach both abstinence and contraception (sometimes called comprehensive sexuality education or abstinence-plus). While the ACLU [American Civil Liberties Union] believes that abstinence is an important component of any educational program about human sexuality, abstinence-only programs raise serious civil liberties and health concerns.

Currently, there are three federal programs dedicated to funding abstinence-only education. Each requires eligible programs to censor critical information that teens—who are or become sexually active—need to protect themselves from STIs and pregnancy.

To receive funds under any of the federal programs, grantees must offer curricula that have as their "exclusive purpose" teaching the benefits of abstinence. In addition, recipients of federal funds may not provide a participating adolescent with any information that is inconsistent with these and similar messages in the same setting as the abstinence program. Consequently, recipients of abstinence-only dollars may not advocate contraceptive use or teach contraceptive methods except to emphasize their failure rates.

Thus, recipients of federal abstinence-only funds operate under a gag order that censors the transmission of vitally needed information. Grantees are forced either to omit any mention of topics such as contraception, abortion, homosexuality, and AIDS or to present these subjects in an incomplete and thus inaccurate fashion.

An independent, federally funded evaluation of the abstinence only education programs authorized under the 1996 welfare reform law concludes that there is "no definitive research [linking] the abstinence education legislation with" the downward trend in "the percentage of teens reporting that they have had sex." Likewise, another . . . study found that while in limited circumstances virginity-pledge programs—which encourage students to make a pledge to abstain from sex until marriage—may delay first intercourse, it also found that virginity pledgers are less likely than nonpledgers to use contraception at first intercourse.

There is ample evidence, however, that programs that include information about both abstinence and contraception reduce sexual risk-taking and pregnancy among teens. Many of these programs have been shown to "delay the onset of sex, reduce the frequency of sex, reduce the number of sexual partners among teens, or increase the use of condoms and other forms of contraception" among sexually active teens. In addition, contrary to claims by proponents of abstinence-only education, sex education curricula that discuss contraception—by presenting accurate information about contraceptive options, effectiveness, and use—do not increase sexual activity. Overall, comprehensive sex education programs have been shown to decrease substantially the risk of STIs and pregnancy among young people.

Abstinence-Only Programs Jeopardize Teen Health

Abstinence-only education is increasingly replacing other forms of sex education in high schools. In 1999, 23 percent of secondary sexuality education teachers taught abstinence as the only way of avoiding STIs and pregnancy, up from 2 percent in 1988. When abstinence-only programs do present information about pregnancy prevention and testing and treatment of sexually transmitted diseases, they do so incompletely and/or inaccurately. For example, one popular program, *Sex Respect*, exaggerates condom failure rates, thereby minimizing their effectiveness in preventing pregnancy and STIs.

Sexually active teens cannot protect themselves from disease and pregnancy without full and accurate information about the transmission of STIs, their treatment, and the effectiveness of contraception. Abstinence-only educational programs jeopardize the health of sexually active teens and leave those who become sexually active at risk for STIs and pregnancy.

Gay and Lesbian Students

Many abstinence-only programs use curricula that dangerously marginalize gay and lesbian students and stigmatize homosexuality. The federal guidelines governing these programs state that they should teach that a "mutually faithful monogamous relationship in [the] context of marriage is the expected standard of human sexual activity." In a society that generally prohibits gays and lesbians from marrying, such a message rejects the idea of sexual intimacy for lesbians and gays and ignores their need for critical information about protecting themselves from STIs in same-sex relationships.

A recent review of the leading abstinence-only curricula found that most address same-sex sexual behavior only within the context of promiscuity and disease, and several are overtly hostile to lesbians and gay men. For example, in its parent-teacher guide, *Facing Reality* instructs educators to teach students that homosexuals with AIDS are now suffering for the "choices" they made regarding their sexual orientation.

By talking only about sex within marriage and teaching about STIs as a form of moral punishment for homosexuality, abstinence-only programs not only undermine efforts to educate students about protecting their health, but create a hostile learning environment for lesbian and gay students.

Many abstinence-only curricula use religious doctrines as guidelines for determining appropriate sexual behavior and values. These curricula violate the First Amendments guarantee of the separation between church and state by using taxpayer money to endorse religious beliefs. A popular abstinence-only curriculum called *Sex Respect*, for example, was originally designed for parochial school use. While it now uses the term "nature" in place of "God," it still has strong religious undertones and references religious publications.

Teens and Oral Sex

While called "abstinence-only," the programs are in essence virginity-based and they pride themselves on not addressing the "graphic terms better left to parents to discuss." In doing so the programs leave the door open for teens to make unsafe sexual choices while operating under the belief that they are still virgins. The ranks of those "saving themselves" by [having oral sex] are increasing as oral sex is on the rise. While oral sex is most prevalent among white teens, it is young black men between 15 and 17 who report the greatest increase in one longitudinal study, jumping from 25 percent in 1988 to 57 percent in 1995, the last year rates were reported in the National Survey of Adolescent Males.

Many teens say that oral sex does not count as sex. Of those who describe themselves as "not sexually active," 13 percent report having oral sex, according to the National Survey of Adolescents and Young Adults. And almost 30 percent of Latino teens consider oral sex to be "safer sex," according to the survey. Nearly half of those who are sexually active consider oral sex the "safer sex." Teens believe oral sex is "not as big a deal" as sexual intercourse. More disturbingly, sexually active girls are twice as likely as sexually active boys to report having had oral sex to avoid intercourse.

Leeche Leong, *Colorlines*, Winter 2004.

Although federal funding guidelines do not permit abstinence-only grantees to convey overt religious messages or to impose religious viewpoints, in practice, many of these programs do precisely that. In 2002, the ACLU challenged the use of taxpayer dollars to support religious activities in the Louisiana Governor's Program (GPA) on Abstinence, a program run on federal and state funds. Over the course of several years, the GPA had funded programs that, among other things, presented "Christ-centered" theater skits, held a religious youth revival, and produced radio shows that "share abstinence as part of the gospel message." A federal district court found that GPA funds were being used to convey religious messages and advance religion, in violation of the Constitution's requirement of separation of church and state. The court ordered Louisiana officials to stop this misuse of taxpayer dollars. The case was on appeal when the parties settled. The GPA agreed to closely monitor the activities of the programs it funds and to stop using GPA dollars to "convey religious messages or otherwise advance religion in any way." Nonetheless, in 2004 the ACLU discovered that the GPA was violating the agreement and directed the state to correct ongoing problems in the program.

Public Opinion

The vast majority of U.S. parents, teachers, and leading medical groups believe that students should receive comprehensive sexuality education.

- In a nationwide poll conducted in 2004 for the Kaiser Family Foundation, National Public Radio, and the Kennedy School of Government, researchers found that an overwhelming majority of parents want sex education curricula to cover topics such as how to use and where to get contraceptives, including codoms; abortion; and sexual orientation.
- A 1999 nationally representative survey of 7th–12th grade teachers in the five specialties most often responsible for sex education found that a strong majority believed that sexuality education courses should cover birth control methods (93.4%), factual information about abortion (89%), where to go for birth control (88.8%), the correct way to use a condom (82%), and sexual orientation (77.8%), among other topics.
- Similarly, major medical organizations have advocated for and/or endorsed comprehensive sexuality education, including the American Medical Association, the American Academy of Pediatrics, the American College of Obstetrics and Gynecology, and the Society for Adolescent Medicine.

"The ostracism faced by many teenage homosexuals forces them to spend even more energy on their own comfort and drives them even further away from family or from citizenship commitments."

Homosexuality Should Be Discussed in High Schools

Bill Boushka

Bill Boushka is an author and the editor of *The Quill* newsletter for gays and lesbians. In the following viewpoint he argues that homosexuality should be taught in an objective way in public schools as would be any other controversial subject. Boushka says the heart of the issue is that many conservatives view homosexuality as an insult to their religious beliefs, but he believes that religious values should be questioned in a democracy. The author also cites several examples where teaching about homosexuality in schools is under attack by conservative groups and government officials.

As you read, consider the following questions:

1. In Boushka's view, what type of statistics are being used by conservatives to justify their belief that gay teens should change their sexual orientation?
2. In what high school class, according to the author, can the gay rights movement be discussed objectively?
3. What is the name of the high school play in which two male characters are attracted to each other and nearly kiss, according to Boushka?

In November 2004, a controversy erupted in upscale Montgomery County, Maryland (next to Washington, D.C.) about a plan to introduce some material about homosexuality into high school curricula, even when not requested by students or parents.

On the surface, it's easy to see the controversy from a libertarian perspective. Public monies should not be used to promote "deviant" or harmful lifestyles. On the other hand, public funds should not be used to advance one particular (conservative) religious view of the world, to encourage discrimination or conformism.

But, given that you have public education, students who are nearing adulthood (let's say 11th and 12th graders, from about age 16 and greater) are certainly entitled to being taught objective and complete information about any socially controversial or divisive topic. Students will find out about such materials from the media (or even my own books and websites) anyway. Students are entitled to learn all of the relevant information about biological and cosmological theories, including evolution, creationism, and intelligent design, in an objective fashion. One cannot be intellectually honest if some topics cannot be spoken about (I am reminded here of a scientist, interviewed in the PBS Nova documentary "Time Travel" who says he now will not speak about time travel!)

This problem, about presenting sexual information honestly, is one that we should work from the inside out, with a sweet opposite field swing. For example, we can start with basic sex education. I don't think there is much argument that for minors sexual abstinence is the safest practice. Minors should not be taught "how" to have sexual intercourse "safely" in public schools unless individual parents have consented. However, whatever medical information is presented should be objective and accurate. Non-monogamous sex (with a non-monogamous partner) always presents some STD [sexually transmitted diseases] (including HIV) risk (as well as pregnancy risk for vaginal intercourse). The risk varies greatly according to the protection used and mechanics and histories of the partners, with the greatest medical risk existing with unprotected anal intercourse. That is simple medical fact, and if presented at all, it should be presented correctly. But all of this skims the surface, because the real debate is about cultural values.

The scientific education could then migrate to the controversy over the extent to which homosexuality is biologically determined—in man and in many animals. This is unsettled, as is the philosophical implication of any outcome.

We can approach the values question from the legal angle, particularly for high school students who have taken enough U.S. history and government to understand important legal concepts: separation of powers, suspect classes, due process of law, the right to privacy and to be left alone. The advanced student should understand some of the legal arguments to defeat sodomy laws, and some of the equal protection thought that could support the idea of gay marriage, even if it seems likely not to go far right now. Certainly advanced placement high school students can understand this material.

Some conservative groups and politicians have been urging school boards to present the viewpoint that homosexuality is chosen and that homosexuals can "change." They sometimes seem really to want the school system to adopt their view, and sometimes use HIV statistics (in the gay male community) as a way to justify their demands that adolescent gays consider "changing." But their real motives seem cultural, and seem aimed to make homosexuality not an acceptable subject in "normal" public interactions or media (particularly as a subject for movies, television, books, etc.) That would be particularly disturbing to me, given my intentions.

Further, "information" about homosexuality is presented as semi-factual instruction, perhaps in ninth or tenth grades in health or biology classes.

Religious Views Are at the Heart of the Issue

This gets us to the real heart of the matter, as to why homosexuality seems so close to tooth pulp for some people. That's culture, values, and the role of the individual in and outside the nuclear family, which has become weaker culturally in recent decades just as individualism has grown. Many conservatives will see the teaching about homosexuality as an affront to their religious values, but that begs the question why religious values cannot be questioned with intellectual candor in a pluralistic society. In fact, academic training in mathematics (the farther you get into differentiation chain rules and integration by parts the better!—and you have to understand what inductive and deductive reasoning—mathematical proof—means in other areas) forces one to think about any problem with intellectual rigor and, yet, openness—we call this facility *critical thinking*. In high school, students vary enormously in their critical thinking skills—which tend to develop as students learn to correlate what they learn in different disciplines (literature, foreign languages, social studies, science, and especially math)—Honors or AP [Advanced Placement Program] students may understand early in high school how to take controversial "information," but less mature students may not get it even when they graduate. Left to a cut-and-dried view of things (often with the influence of how religion affects thinking in cultural areas) these same conservatives will see instruction about homosexuality as subversive to their whole psychological investment in the nuclear family, which they see as inimical to their sense of self-worth and security. To many people, family responsibility is the way you first earn your place in the world, and family responsibility, when carried out, provides a way not only to raise children but also to take care of dependent adults and honored elders. Many people depend totally on their place in the family for self-worth and have little sense of personal initiative outside of biologically assigned blood family. To teach about homosexuality would seem to be an invitation to teens to go out and desert your family to do your own thing for your own individual happiness, to follow your own chosen goals. The ostracism faced by many teenage homosexuals forces them to spend even more energy on their own comfort and drives them even further away from family or from citizenship commitments that society normally supports. Now complaints about the losses to family sounds like whining and an admission of insecurity, but many people see the family as something that doesn't work unless everyone participates (and that includes taking part in providing children and lineage from your own blood if at all possible). Of course, political science teaches us how the Left looks at the family as a

Poll Identifies Gay Students

The Gay, Lesbian and Straight Education Network (GLSEN) today [October 7, 2004] announced results from a new national poll on students' attitudes on sexual orientation. Based on results from the poll, approximately 5% of America's high school students identify as lesbian or gay, 16% of America's students have a gay or lesbian family member, and 72% know someone who is gay or lesbian.

The national poll conducted by Widmeyer Research and Polling in conjunction with Penn, Schoen & Berland Associates, Inc., asked questions of 9th–12th grade students across the country about sexual orientation, name-calling, and general attitudes towards lesbian and gay people in schools.

"The findings suggest that, on average, every classroom in America has at least one student who identifies as lesbian or gay and that a majority of those students know at least one gay or lesbian person, whether it be a teacher, a classmate or a family member," noted GLSEN Executive Director Kevin Jennings.

Key findings from the national poll include:

- *Anti-gay language is rampant.* 66% of students report using homophobic language, such as "that's so gay" to describe something that is wrong, bad or stupid; 81% report hearing homophobic language in their schools frequently or often.

- *Nearly 3/4 of high school students know a gay or lesbian person.* 48% of students know a lesbian or gay classmate; 30% have a close lesbian or gay friend; 11% know a lesbian or gay teacher.

- *Parents, friends and family influence students' attitudes most.* 65% of students identify their personal experiences with gay people as an important influence in their attitudes about gay people; 58% note the important role their parents play while 28% acknowledge the important role of television with gay characters.

Press Release from the Gay, Lesbian and Straight Education Network, October 7, 2004. www.glsen.org.

---

transmitter of unearned wealth and privilege and as an easy cover for personal corruption at the top.

The reason why this whole family responsibility thing is so timely now is that it fits into a larger debate about the obligations of *citizenship* in a world that seems increasingly troubled and threatened, and in which individual freedom must not be taken for granted. A world that faces global warming, oil shocks, terrorism, and worldwide competition for resources may be a world that demands more shared sacrifice in the future than that experienced by recent generations (since the end of Vietnam). One way to make the world more stable is to make sure that individuals, in expressing their freedoms, show accountability to others and "pay their dues." Into this discussion comes concern about falling birthrates, retirement, and how an increasing elderly population can be cared for. Discussions about filial responsibility (derivative of family responsibility) are bound to come back, sometimes in conjunction with proposals about community service and even national service.

Discrimination Adds to the Controversy

The fact is that a free society requires sharing of some responsibilities, in all sorts of ways, ranging from defense (military service and law enforcement), to blood and organ donations, to participation in childcare and giving attention to the disabled and caring for the elderly, as well as careful thought about the personal use of possibly limited resources. The argument can be made that the "gay lifestyle" (particularly for men) inhibits sharing these responsibilities. But then so can the argument made that these constrictions are circular in nature and come from discriminatory laws (the military "don't ask don't tell" policy or worse, the refusal in most states to recognize gay marriages or even civil unions, the prohibition in some states against gay adoptions, the strict blood donation policy even for HIV negative gay men). Then the discussion winds down, in annotation, to the cultural importance of connecting sex to procreation, marriage and babies. People (like me) who do not participate in that game are at a distinct disadvantage.

The school systems (as well as campuses) may be the best place for a spirited debate on the "real" citizenship problems. Some of the material naturally occurs in objective settings in standard high school courses, like biology (where pathogens are presented and STDs can be introduced, and even the scientific concepts underlying retroviruses like HIV can be presented), and social studies, where the gay rights movement can be presented briefly and objectively, at least, as a sequel to the civil rights movement of the 1960s. At a certain point, school systems get caught in the vise between rationalism and religion (as some people experience faith), and this conflict affects other areas such as evolution and the teaching of other topics in history. The underlying philosophical problems tend not to get addressed until college. After all, graduate students still write dissertations on this battle. In the meantime, the best students in public high schools rightly and cynically suspect that information on critical social and biological science topics is being dumbed down and politicized for the "common good" (particularly overprotection of children) especially in the political climate of "No Child Left Behind." What students need, of course, is the skills (and the freedom) to get the rest of the information themselves and start connecting the dots. These skills cannot come too early.

Teaching About Gay Issues Is Under Attack

Maria Glod, "School's Official Assails 'Gay Lifestyle', Fairfax Letter Urges Revisions to Teaching," *The Washington Post*, Feb. 3, 2005, p. B1, reports that Fairfax County School Board member Stephen M. Hunt sent letters on private stationery to 24 Fairfax County high school principals, in which he urged the school system to provide speakers with an "ex-gay" perspective to present the view that "homosexuality is a choice and 'a very destructive lifestyle.'" Hunt's letter was not reviewed by the other 12 school board members and represents only his own views. Hunt notes that his letter says "that students should respect the rights of gay peers. 'If a person does choose a gay lifestyle, we should respect their freedom, their safety and their choice.'" According to NBC4 in Washington (Feb. 3 2005), the school district presents (1) sexual orientation as innate (2) sexual behavior as chosen (3) abstinence as the safest behavior for teenagers still in high school. . . . There seems to me to be an ethical issue of conflict of interest rules. If Hunt is a public official (or in a position where he can speak for an organization besides himself), he should go through channels in making a controversial proposal, rather than going public on his own in order to create a stir.

Another good way to look at this problem is to ask, what if a school board member wanted to present the view (subjunctive mood!) that Jews and Muslims can't go to Heaven, under the guise of teaching "World History"? But, then again, school boards need to be able to take up almost any culturally controversial information in an orderly manner in deciding how to present it to students.

Anderson. © by Kirk Anderson. Reproduced by permission.

I will provide here what The Citizens' Advisory Committee on Family Life and Human Development, Montgomery County, MD, repeats from the CDC [Centers for Disease Control and Prevention] ". . . according to the U.S. Centers for Disease Control and Prevention, 'Among young men 13–24 years, 49 percent of all AIDS cases reported in 2000 were among men who have sex with men' and '9 percent were among young men infected heterosexually.'" Among infected males, this statistic actually shows a slow but inevitable increase in heterosexual transmission (relative to homosexual transmission) in the United States (as compared to Africa) over the years. This was reported in a Letter to the Editor, "Risky Business," *The Washington Times*, February 8, 2005, p. A16. This letter seemed to be aimed at the idea of promoting in the public schools the possibility that homosexuals can choose to "change." Of course, however, many individuals manage lifestyles with increased risks well on their own; what happens to those who can't?

On Feb 9, 2005 NBC4 reported that a high school (Stone Bridge in Ashburn) in London County, VA had performed a play by Sabrina Audrey Jess, *Offsides* in which two male football characters (allegedly) nearly kiss and may experience homosexual attraction; apparently this has caused a controversy among some parents and politicians. Michael Lewis and Karen Brulliard provide an account, "Gay Themed High School Play Sparks Va. Protests" on Feb. 9, 2005 in *The Washington Post*. According to the story, "Del. Richard H. Black (R-Loudoun) e-mailed his supporters claiming that, in the play, 'two male students engaged in a homosexual kiss onstage' and that public schools were 'being used to promote a homosexual lifestyle.' His son-in-law, Loudoun County Supervisor Mick Staton Jr. (R-Sugarland Run), followed up with a missive of his own, warning of the play's disturbing "indoctrination." On Sunday [Feb. 13, 2005], activists blanketed Loudoun churches with fliers decrying the production." However, more accurate accounts of the 20-minute play say that the lights dim before the kiss, which is not seen explicitly.

In May 2005, Montgomery County, MD announced that it would implement a voluntary health education program in selected middle and high schools (and next school year in all schools) that explains condoms and presents homosexual orientation in an objective manner. Some "conservative" parents (the two groups are Citizens for a Responsible Curriculum, and Parents and Friends of Ex-gays and Gays) have filed suit on First Amendment grounds, claiming that kids who opt out (and who support religious-based ex-gay views) would stand out and be stigmatized as "religious," or "irrational," or "intolerant." Jon Ward, "Parents file suit to stop sex-ed: Call new class indoctrination," *The Washington Times*, May 4, 2005 (and on May 5, a front-page headline, "Sex-ed program pulled from year's curriculum"). U.S. District Judge Alexander Williams put the program on hold, and the school system agreed to take it back and review it.

In May 2005, Walter Jones (R-NC) introduced a bill in

the House to withdraw federal education funds from states where school boards don't establish "parental advisory boards" to review books and other materials published by school libraries. The bill is called the Parental Empowerment Act of 2005 (H.R. 2295). The bill was apparently motivated by the appearance of a novel *King & King* at Wilmington, NC school libraries (a fairy tale in which two princes get married). . . .

On June 9, 2005, Michael Janofsjy, "Gay Rights Battlefields Spread to Public Schools," *The New York Times*, p A18, maintains that conservative groups have been emboldened by what happened with gay marriage (esp. in Ohio) in the 2004 elections. There is a bill in Alabama to prevent state spending on any materials that promote the homosexual lifestyle, a bill in Oklahoma to require public libraries to restrict access to children to gay materials, and a similar measure proposed in Louisiana. I suppose these measures could eventually affect what publishers will buy. The principal at East Bakersfield High School (CA) declined to allow a series on gay issues to be published out of security concerns (a judge had recommended anonymous publication, which I personally consider unethical).

> "*An ethic of sexual anarchy with homosexuality as its lead issue is being deliberately sold to our youth under the guise of 'safety' and 'tolerance.'*"

Homosexuality Should Not Be Discussed in High Schools

Linda P. Harvey

Linda P. Harvey is president of Choice for Truth, a project of Mission: America, a conservative evangelical advocacy group. In this viewpoint Harvey argues that public high schools are being used to indoctrinate students into homosexuality. Gay-friendly teachers are distorting historical facts in order to promote positive views about homosexuals, she contends. For example, one teacher erroneously claimed that Alexander the Great was gay. Moreover, according to Harvey, teachers who are openly gay could sexually molest students and are bad role models. Harvey also argues that gay student support groups at high schools are used by older teens to lure younger students into having sex with them.

As you read, consider the following questions:

1. According to Harvey, how many high schools have gay-straight alliance clubs?
2. The author states that a high school student from Minnesota was suspended for wearing a shirt that had what phrase on it?
3. What is Harvey's view on the connection between sexual orientation and genetics?

Pink triangles in classrooms. Grade school studies of "gay" history. Transvestite speakers. School-wide events to celebrate homosexuality. Student activists spreading propaganda through school publications. Legislation mandating homosexual indoctrination.

This was the school year 2000–2001. What will our neighborhood schools be doing this fall to support the relentless agenda of homosexual activists?

In the Massachusetts town of Newton, home of homosexual congressman Barney Frank, a high school history teacher taught that Alexander the Great was a "gay" man. Other teachers in Massachusetts are building lessons around the Stonewall Inn riots in Greenwich Village in 1969, an event credited by homosexual activists with kicking off the "gay rights" movement. In a third grade music class in a Massachusetts town, the male teacher told the children Tchaikovsky was a homosexual, and that society's "homophobia" prompted his suicide.

Newton North High School sponsored a special "To Be Gay" day, complete with inaccurate brochures heavily promoting transgendered behaviors (cross-dressing, having surgery to alter one's biological sex, etc.).

All of this is taking place in a state where 156 schools host homosexual clubs, called "gay-straight alliances" by advocates. Such clubs are provided seed money by a state program to "support" students practicing homosexual behavior. Nationally, GLSEN has said there are over 800 such clubs. GLSEN, the Gay Lesbian and Straight Education Network, was founded in Massachusetts in the early 1990s by a male teacher engaged in homosexual activity.

In California, meanwhile, a week . . . at Santa Rosa High School was devoted to "Days of Diversity." Skits promoted homosexual and heterosexual promiscuous sex. One skit derided the Bible by implication, when a student actor who believed in a special "book" that she reads on Sunday, said that this book gave her permission to "hate." Parents were not fully informed about the contents of the workshops, and many feel they were deceived.

Younger children in another Marin County school saw a performance troupe called "Cootie Shots," whose skits depict families consisting of two mommies and two daddies. This group gains entry to schools by saying it offers programs on "tolerance and diversity." But their version of diversity is really cleverly packaged deviance. In one of the group's skits, the fairy-tale character Rapunzel cuts off her long hair and runs away with her girlfriend.

The high school students also presented skits dealing with sexual molestation, rape, anorexia and suicide. Other workshops during this diversity week advocated radical environmentalism, socialism and animal rights. Some parents who had submitted the "opt-out" forms provided through California pro-family organizations had children who still attended the events. Legal action is being pursued by some of these parents against the school.

Gays Want Opponents Silenced

And California faces even more problems if current legislation passes. After the passage of state law . . . mandating diversity field trips and other pro-homosexual school activity, [the] legislature is considering SB 225,[1] which would require that schools with interscholastic sports teams adopt non-discrimination codes supporting "sexual orientation" as well as "perceived gender," or risk being banned from the California Interscholastic Federation. This reaches into the private school sector, which of course has been the goal of the activists all along. Nothing will satisfy until *all* of society is supportive of homosexuality. A second bill, SB 257, would force schools to target speech that opposes homosexuality as being discriminatory and equivalent to harassment.

It's not just the liberal northeast and the "left coast" of California where these atrocities are being forced on children. At a high school near St. Paul, Minnesota, 16-year old Elliott Chambers was suspended when he wore a sweatshirt to school . . . that said "Straight Pride" on the front. On the back was a sketch of a man and woman holding hands. Some students complained to the principal that they were offended.

Elliot says he had no idea the shirt would cause such an uproar. He had ordered it from a web site (straightpride.com)

1. The bill became law in October 2001.

after someone had seen it at a political rally in the fall. He just thought it was "cool." After months of pro-homosexual indoctrination in his high school, he had quietly developed a dislike for the climate of bias.

Gay Sex Ed Is Attacked

A new sex education program for 8th and 10th graders in Montgomery County, Md., public schools is being attacked by conservatives for allegedly advancing a homosexual agenda. The chairman of the advisory committee that drew up the sex education curriculum is a homosexual activist whose writings on a religious website include, "Gay Marriage, A Jewish Perspective."

The revised curriculum, will be piloted in three county middle schools and three high schools in mid-April [2005] and then evaluated in June. The curriculum calls for, among other things, a condom demonstration video and information about "sexual variation."

Steve Fisher, spokesman for the newly formed Citizens for a Responsible Curriculum, told *Cybercast News Service* that the new Montgomery County curriculum is pro-homosexual and would unfairly ask students to examine their sexuality.

"One of the things the new curriculum is proposing to do is to encourage children as early as 13 to self-identify their sexual preference in school," Fisher said. "The new curriculum is essentially saying that same-sex experimentation and play among adolescence is normal and should not be discouraged."

He described the new curriculum as a "blatant attempt to make sure that the only information that was going to be provided to the teachers as far as resources and background information was [pro-homosexual]."

Fisher said attempts by some of the members on the Montgomery County Board of Education's advisory committee "to balance the information with recommendations from other organizations like various mainstream churches" were denied. Instead, he said, the curriculum was "pushed through pretty much without a whole lot of exposure or discussion from the parents."

Kathleen Rhodes, "Sex Ed Revisions Blasted for Alleged Pro-Homosexual Bias," CNSNews.com. March 10, 2005. www.cnsnews.com.

"In our school, there are 50 regular classrooms that have been marked with pink triangles as 'safe' zones," Elliott says.

The "safe zone" signate lists the name of a teacher as a resource. The idea is that students who have questions about their sexuality can go to this teacher "safely"—in other words, knowing the teacher will be uncritical, even supportive of homosexuality. The procedure is that these teachers then refer the questioning student to a pro-homosexual counselor outside the school or an activist group like PFLAG [Parents and Friends of Lesbians and Gays], Elliott told us. This all happens without parental notification or consent.

But the atmosphere doesn't end with promotion, but also includes intimidation. Some Woodbury students have been given detentions if they use the phrase, "That's so gay," as an expression of distaste.

Yet teachers are free to express strong opinions as they wish, especially about Christianity. After a "holiday" concert at the school [one] Christmas season, one female math teacher opened a discussion about the song content, which was dominated by Christian songs. "Didn't you feel discriminated against?" she pointedly asked one Muslim girl.

Apparently, the school board of Woodbury High School as well as the PTA [Parent-Teachers Association] knew nothing about the pink triangles until the publicity surrounding Elliott's case. The "safe zone" program was an idea implemented by a male librarian along with the principal. After the case surfaced, the triangles were modified to add symbols to racial and religious equality as well as equality for those with disabilities.

Elliott's parents, Lena and Kendal Chambers, have sued the school district for its stubborn stance. In a preliminary injunction . . . , a U.S. District court judge ruled in favor of the Chambers, saying there is "a strong likelihood" that the principal infringed upon Elliott's constitutional rights.[2]

Yet it could be worse. There are as yet no openly "gay" teachers at the school who might pose a risk to students as poor role models, or worse—the threat of sexual molestation. People who profess a homosexual preference are much more likely to molest children and adolescents, especially males. A Newton, Massachusetts parent told us that at his

2. The U.S. District Court in St. Paul, Minnesota, made the injunction permanent.

child's elementary school, all five of the male teachers are openly homosexual. He believes this shows a clear preference in hiring.

Gay Teens Promote Myths

There are, meanwhile, at schools throughout the country, student activists co-opting school publications to disseminate the myths of homosexual advocacy. They use the budding journalist's pen to claim it's an issue of "enlightenment and education" and a civil rights matter rather than well-documented unsafe behavior. At Upper Arlington High School in Columbus [Ohio] . . . students devoted ten pages of a slick magazine to an inaccurate and one-sided promotion of homosexuality. The advocacy was laced with the usual claims of "prejudice and ignorance" by conservatives. It also inaccurately portrayed the work of the ex-gay ministry Exodus International. . . .

An entire column also promoted a Columbus community "support" group for "gay, lesbian, bisexual and transgendered" youth under 21. This group meets in a homosexual church, and even young teens can attend without parental notification or consent. Such groups exist throughout the country in most metropolitan areas, posing a high risk to children who can interact, socialize and be lured into sexual episodes by the older teens and adults who operate such groups.

An ethic of sexual anarchy with homosexuality as its lead issue is being deliberately sold to our youth under the guise of "safety" and "tolerance." Meanwhile, young people's lives and emotional stability are endangered if they make a decision in these tender years to engage in homosexual activity—or are seduced into such acts by a teacher, coach, or older peer. As we have repeatedly said, there is no evidence of a genetic connection for homosexual desires, and a wealth of evidence that such feelings arise from emotional instability, often fueled by the confused legacy of sexual abuse. The thousands of ex-homosexuals testify to the fact that homosexual feelings can be changed, and it is a betrayal of our children not to let them know about this hope. Yet many schools now are being told by activist groups, including the ACLU [American Civil Liberties Union] and teacher organizations, that they must not encourage heterosexuality instead of homosexuality when counseling troubled or questioning kids.

The "gay"-friendly educational system continues to open its doors to groups like GLSEN and PFLAG, who have been aided by substantial funding boosts in recent years. Many concerned parents are removing their children from the public schools. But others, equally concerned, either do not have the option because of family circumstances, or have no clear educational alternative for their children. And, should we abandon the schools anyway?

Turning our backs on the culture and retreating into conservative or religious enclaves is what got us into this mess to begin with. Let's contact our local schools, find out what's going on, and join with other concerned citizens to make some changes this next school year.

"Beyond mutual lifelong monogamy among uninfected couples, condom use is the only method for reducing the risk of HIV infection and STDs available to sexually active individuals."

Teaching About Condoms Can Prevent Sexually Transmitted Diseases

Heather Boonstra

In the following viewpoint Heather Boonstra asserts that socially conservative Republicans in Congress are erroneously claiming that condoms are ineffective in preventing the spread of HIV and other sexually transmitted diseases (STDs). While the author grants that condoms are not infallible, they are highly effective in preventing transmission of STDs, she contends. Boonstra also argues that relying on abstinence-only education programs—which do not include discussions of condom use—will lead to an increase in STDs. Boonstra is a senior public policy associate with the Alan Guttmacher Institute, a liberal think tank.

As you read, consider the following questions:

1. What two STDs, according to Boonstra, did a National Institutes of Health panel declare that condoms were effective in preventing?
2. In the author's opinion, what type of study is needed to adequately test the effectiveness of condoms against STD transmission?

Heather Boonstra, "Public Health Advocates Say Campaigning to Disparage Condoms Threatens STD Prevention Efforts," *The Guttmacher Report*, vol. 6, March 2003, pp. 1–6. Copyright © 2004 by The Alan Guttmacher Institute. Reproduced by permission.

In 1999, social conservatives in Congress initiated a new strategy to further their moral agenda of promoting abstinence outside of marriage as official government policy—claiming that condoms do not protect against sexually transmitted diseases (STDs). Led by then-Rep. Tom Coburn (R-OK), a physician and staunch proabstinence opponent of government-funded family planning programs, they were successful in attaching an amendment to the House version of the Breast and Cervical Cancer Treatment Act mandating that condom packages carry a cigarette-type warning that condoms offer "little or no protection" against an extremely common STD, human papillomavirus (HPV), some strains of which cause cervical cancer. Although this directive was removed before the bill was enacted, Coburn and his allies were able to secure a requirement that the Food and Drug Administration (FDA) reexamine condom labels to determine whether they are medically accurate with respect to condoms' "effectiveness or lack of effectiveness" in STD prevention. . . .

At the behest of Coburn and other condom critics, NIH [The National Institutes of Health] in June 2000 convened a panel of experts for a two-day workshop to examine the body of evidence on the effectiveness of condoms in preventing the transmission of eight STDs: HIV, gonorrhea, chlamydia, syphilis, chancroid, trichomoniasis, genital herpes and HPV. The panel considered 138 peer-reviewed articles in all. It determined that "condition-specific" studies were sufficiently methodologically strong to warrant a *definitive* conclusion only for HIV and gonorrhea. Accordingly, in its carefully worded summary report issued in July 2001, the panel concluded that consistent and correct condom use prevents (in addition, of course, to pregnancy) transmission of HIV between women and men and gonorrhea transmission from women to men. Beyond that, the panel concluded, the published epidemiologic literature is insufficient to warrant definitive statements specific to the other six STDs considered by the panel.

That there are insufficient studies specific to the six other STDs reviewed by the panel to warrant a *definitive* statement does not mean, however, that no assumptions can be made about the protective effect of condoms with regard to those diseases. Indeed, a critical conclusion in the workshop summary report that largely has been overlooked is that condoms are "essentially impermeable" to even the smallest of STD viruses. Based on that finding—that "studies . . . have demonstrated that condoms provide a highly effective barrier to the transmission of particles of similar size to those of the smallest STD virus"—two important assumptions can be made and, in fact, are made in the workshop report itself. The first is that there is a "strong probability of condom effectiveness" against so-called discharge diseases that, as with HIV, are transmitted by genital secretions, such as semen or vaginal fluids. Included here would be chlamydia and trichomoniasis in addition to gonorrhea. The second is, once again, that there is "a strong probability of condom effectiveness" against infections that are transmitted through "skin-to-skin" contact—provided, however, that the source of the infection is in an area that is covered or protected by the condom. Three "genital ulcer diseases"—genital herpes, syphilis and chancroid—as well as HPV fall in this category. All can occur in genital areas that are covered or protected by condoms, but they also can occur in areas that are not. Therefore, correct condom use would be expected to protect against transmission of genital ulcer diseases and HPV in some, but not all, instances.

The report goes on to raise a number of methodological challenges that make it difficult to study the effectiveness of condoms against specific STDs. The ideal study, a randomized controlled clinical trial, has not been used because it would require control-group participants to be counseled not to use condoms. Such counseling is not considered ethically acceptable—itself an implicit acknowledgement of condom effectiveness in STD prevention within the scientific community. As a result of these standards for study design, none of the studies reviewed by the workshop panel was considered optimal, and any future studies will face similar challenges. . . .

Condoms the Key to STD Prevention

HIV and STD prevention advocates acknowledge that condoms are not "perfect." They note that the current FDA

[Food and Drug Administration] labeling now under review [as of 2005] does likewise, advising consumers that when used properly, latex condoms will help reduce the risk of HIV and other STDs, although no method can guarantee 100% protection. Still, they say, condoms must remain a key component of HIV and STD prevention efforts both in the United States and globally because, in the words of the workshop summary itself, "Beyond mutual lifelong monogamy among uninfected couples, condom use is the only method for reducing the risk of HIV infection and STDs available to sexually active individuals."

Abstinence Is Not Reducing STD Rates

Teens who pledge to remain virgins until marriage have the same rates of sexually transmitted diseases as those who don't pledge abstinence, according to a study that examined the sex lives of 12,000 adolescents.

Those who make a public pledge to abstain until marriage delay sex, have fewer sex partners and get married earlier, according to the data, gathered from adolescents ages 12 to 18 who were questioned again six years later. But the two groups' STD rates were statistically similar.

The problem, the study found, is that those virginity "pledgers" are much less likely to use condoms.

"Study: Abstinence Pledges Not Reducing Rates of STDs," *USA Today*, March 9, 2004.

In that light, experts in the field say efforts to promote abstinence by disparaging condoms are misguided because they could increase the likelihood that people will fail to use condoms when they do have sex, thus putting themselves at unnecessary risk. "It is hard enough to convince people who choose to have sex—even those who are at high risk of HIV—to use condoms," says David Harvey, executive director of the AIDS Alliance for Children, Youth and Families. "The last thing we need is the government promoting the idea that condoms do no good. This approach will undermine the gains we have made and result in more people with HIV and other sexually transmitted infections."

STD expert Ward Cates, president of Family Health Institute, contends that intentionally undermining public confidence in the effectiveness of condoms is not justified as a matter of science. He says the fact that insufficient data exist to prove definitively that condoms protect against some STDs—while technically true—has created an opening allowing condom opponents to claim that condoms are inadequate. "While I'm impressed with the thoroughness and accuracy of the . . . report, its emphasis on condom failures can be distorted," Cates says. "By such dwelling on the failures, the successes of male condoms are obscured, and the method is unnecessarily tainted," he wrote. "From a public health perspective, the data clearly show that the glass is 90% full (that condoms are relatively effective) and only 10% empty (that data are inadequate)." In an interview Cates adds, "Thus, the question should not be whether condoms work if used (they do!), but rather what is the appropriate role of condoms in comprehensive HIV prevention programs."

All of this leads Jacqueline E. Darroch, The Alan Guttmacher Institute's vice president for science, to question the need for a great deal more biomedical research to clarify condom effectiveness against individual STDs. "We already know that latex condoms do successfully prevent transmission of most STDs, but that their effectiveness depends in large part on how consistently and correctly they are used," Darroch says. "What health educators and service providers really need from research is a better understanding of the difficulties people face using condoms effectively, so that they can better help sexually active couples wanting to avoid disease or unintended pregnancy to use condoms consistently and correctly at every act of intercourse. Our goal should be programs that reinforce this message and that get through to people who are having sex and are at risk for STDs in an unequivocal way the news that condoms are a necessary and effective way to prevent infection."

> *"Condoms, the only form of birth control purported to stop disease and the spread of STDs, don't work."*

Teaching About Condoms Cannot Prevent Sexually Transmitted Diseases

Meg Meeker

Meg Meeker is a pediatrician, author, and lecturer on teen issues. In this viewpoint she argues that condoms offer little or no protection against sexually transmitted diseases, especially the human papillomavirus (HPV). Meeker states that condoms have lulled teens into a false sense of safety, and she notes that while condom use has increased among teens, so has the rate of STDs. She concludes that using condoms can no longer be considered a safe-sex practice.

As you read, consider the following questions:
1. According to Meeker, how many high schools in the United States make condoms available to students?
2. Condoms work best in preventing the spread of what disease, in the author's view?
3. What do teens believe, according to Meeker, is the best way to prevent the spread of STDs?

Meg Meeker, *Epidemic: How Teen Sex Is Killing Our Kids.* Washington, DC: Lifeline Press, 2002. Copyright © 2002 by Lifeline Press.

W here sexual health is concerned, the nation is full of condom-mania. Even as parents and educators wring their hands over adolescent pregnancy and STDs [sexually transmitted diseases], many grin with relief and hold up a slim foil packet as the "solution." (I see this at every conference I attend.) An estimated 400 high schools in the United States make condoms available to students. And many kids are using them.

Indeed, condom use by adolescents has skyrocketed during the past 20 years. Condom use among teens has increased from about 21% among sexually active boys ages 17 to 19 to nearly 67% in 1995. Other data from 1997 shows that about half of adolescent girls in grades nine through twelve said they used a condom during their last sexual intercourse, compared with just over one-third in 1991.

In a way, we might view all this as a victory. After all, there has been a slight drop in the number of teenage pregnancies.

But the problem is this: *During that same time period, the number of cases of kids with STDs has grown to epidemic proportions.*

Condoms, the only form of birth control purported to stop disease and the spread of STDs, *don't work.* "Safe" sex isn't safe. And the epidemic of STDs is due in part to this overconfident reliance on condoms. . . .

So why aren't condoms doing the job they're supposed to do? . . . You need to know, for the sake of your own teens, the difference between fact and hype where condoms are concerned. Unfortunately, that means repeating some bad news: *Condoms are no solution.*

I can hear your objections already: "No solution? What about 'safe sex'"?

During the 1990s, these two words became the mantra of health educators in schools and health care clinics for teens across the country, and code words for using condoms. But how do we know that condoms are safe? And what does "safe" mean? We must be clear about definitions, because I'm a stickler for making sure that both teens and parents understand the risks.

The term "safe" means that a person won't get harmed or sick. And so does the word "protected." So when we tell teens that the way to have "safe sex" is to use condoms, which are perceived as "protection," we're implying that they'll be protected from harm and disease. So that's what they hear: If they use condoms, nothing bad like STDs or pregnancy will happen to them.

Medically, however, this just isn't true. The best that condoms can do is *reduce* a person's risk for contracting disease. Even if condoms are used perfectly, 100% of the time, risk still exists. That risk is that the condom will slip or break about 2 to 4% of the time. And that's just the beginning. We also have to factor in what disease the condom is supposed to prevent. Gonorrhea? Syphilis? HPV? HIV? The risk of getting any one of these differs with a condom. The truth is, condoms do best in reducing the risk of HIV, but they're much worse with many other STDs. . . . The levels of safety are much lower than you think.

I have a problem with the word "safe." It makes kids feel that they won't get pregnant or catch a disease if they use condoms. But it's not true. We need to tell kids that reducing the risks is not the same as being safe. We need to tell them exactly what the risks are, and what condoms can and cannot do. We must be honest with our kids. It could save their lives.

How much do condoms really reduce the risk of our kids becoming infected with disease? Our best information comes from a panel of 28 medical experts in a recent report sponsored by the National Institutes of Health. The group comprised men and women, practicing physicians and researchers, liberals and conservatives, all trained to have their fingers on the pulse of the spread and prevention of STDs in the United States. They gathered for a two-day workshop in Herndon, Virginia, in June 2000, to evaluate the effectiveness of condoms. Thirteen months later they released their findings.

They concluded that, while male latex condoms could reduce the transmission of HIV/AIDS, there was *not enough evidence to determine that they were effective in reducing the risk of most other sexually transmitted diseases.*

The report unleashed a firestorm of reaction, with numerous physicians' groups and members of Congress calling for the immediate resignation of then-CDC director Dr. Jeffrey Koplan, for hiding and misrepresenting vital medical information that showed condoms don't fully protect against STD transmission. "The failure of public health efforts to prevent the STD epidemic in America is related to the CDC's 'safe-sex' promotion and its attempts to withhold from the American people the truth of condom ineffectiveness," group members said.

Tell Teens the Truth About Condoms

Much was made in the media recently about a study concluding that distributing condoms in schools does not increase sexual activity among young people. But what's being missed is that distributing those condoms isn't keeping young people safe from diseases that can change their lives forever. This doesn't mean condoms should play no role in the battle against HIV and STDs [sexually transmitted diseases], they just shouldn't play the central role—especially for kids.

The only way to keep young people safe is to tell them the truth—about STDs and condoms. And tell them we know they are capable of, and we expect them to, avoid sexual activity. Most people don't realize it, but today a majority of high school students do not have sex and the numbers are growing. . . .

The government did a dangerous disservice to America's teens when it incorrectly called condoms "highly effective." Research shows that the only way young people can be safe from an STD epidemic is to wait. Fortunately, more and more teens are making just that choice.

Shepherd Smith, "The Truth Must Get to Teens About STDs," The Institute for Youth Development, March 1, 2004. www.youthdevelopment.org.

Unfortunately, this firestorm quickly died down. Today if you ask most adults (or teens) about the best way to prevent STDs, they will answer with one smug word: condoms.

They're wrong. . . .

For decades we've been giving the same time-honored advice to young men who are coming of age: If you're going to have sex, at least use a condom. You'll hit a double-header—protection against unwanted pregnancies and defense against disease.

It was a powerful argument, and our boys listened. Teens themselves are more frightened of pregnancy than disease because, from their perspective, a baby will disrupt their lives more than an infection—particularly an infection that has no symptoms and may not cause harm until "years down the road."

As difficult as it can be to make a teen understand the consequences of sexual behaviors, it is easier to help them appreciate the reality of teen pregnancy than the reality of the STD epidemic. First, teens hear more about pregnancy. We have been on the bandwagon of curbing teen pregnancy longer than we've been trying to stop teen STDs. In short, teens are more aware because we've educated them.

Second, teens can't see infections, but they can see a swollen belly. They can see a girl at school growing large with pregnancy. Unfortunately, most times, teens who have an STD or two don't have symptoms. This doesn't help them or us because they live with infections they don't realize they have, and don't seek treatment.

Third, teens are often egocentric. Pregnancy puts them out. It can't be cured with a shot of antibiotic or a handful of pills. Babies force teens to make tough decisions. They require a total lifestyle change. Teens can grasp the reality of that. All of this makes teens respect pregnancy more—and fear it more—than STDs.

Finally, teens don't want to let their parents down or get them upset. Telling a parent that she has an infection is easier for many teens than telling a parent she's pregnant. Again, this relates to a fear. Fear of telling mom or dad motivates some teens to prevent pregnancy rather than STDs if any preventative measures are to be taken at all. . . .

News of the STD epidemic shocks us all. And once you understand that condoms don't keep our kids safe, the news can seem even more overwhelming. But we must deal with it head-on. Condoms have lulled us into complacency too long. They have provided a stopgap measure that can no longer hold back the flood of STDs. Our reliance on condoms has played a key role in the spread of disease, along with the major influences of the media and the new sexual habits of kids.

Periodical Bibliography

The following articles have been selected to supplement the diverse views presented in this chapter.

Chris Brown	"Should Schools Permit Condom Machines?" *Liverpool Daily Post*, May 14, 2004.
Hannah Brücker and Peter Bearman	"After the Promise: The STD Consequences of Adolescent Virginity Pledges," *Journal of Adolescent Health*, April 2005.
Margery Eagan	"Old Adult Taboo No Match for Teen Cynicism," *Boston Herald*, February 22, 2005.
Michael Foust	"Are Public Schools the Next Battleground over Homosexuality?" *Baptist Press News*, June 7, 2005.
Alison George	"Teenagers Special: Going All the Way," *New Scientist*, March 5, 2005.
Bonnie L. Halpern-Felsher	"Adolescents' Self-Efficacy to Communicate About Sex: It's Role in Condom Attitudes, Commitment, and Use," *Adolescence*, Fall 2004.
Stephen Hanson	"Heads I Win; Tails Don't Count: The Actual Value of Abstinence," *Free Inquiry*, February/March 2004.
Joy Lanzendorfer	"It's 10 p.m., Do You Know? Kids Aren't Having Casual Sex, They're Having Oral Sex," *North Bay Bohemian*, October 17, 2002.
Todd Melby	"Making Radical Changes in Sexuality Education," *Contemporary Sexuality*, November 2004.
Karen Kay Perrin	"Abstinence-Only Education: How We Got Here and Where We're Going," *Journal of Public Health Policy*, 2003.
Elizabeth Querna	"Teaching Teens About Sex: Virginity Pledges May Not Protect Adolescents from STDs," *U.S. News & World Report*, March 21, 2005.
Kandra Strauss	"The Birds, the Bees, Oh My!" *NEA Today*, April 2003.
James Wagoner	"New CDC Data on Teens and Oral Sex," September 15, 2005. www.advocatesforyouth.org.

For Further Discussion

Chapter 1

1. Jane D. Brown argues that the way that teen sex is portrayed in teen magazines, television, movies, and music helps shape how adolescents perceive sex. Do you agree with this assessment? If so, in what ways have the mass media influenced your attitudes about sex?

2. Kaveri Subrahmanyam, Patricia M. Greenfield, and Brendesha Tynes say that the Internet, especially teen chat rooms, has become an important source of information for teens about sex. Have you ever used a teen chat room? What was discussed in the room the first time you were there? Did you feel comfortable or uncomfortable with the discussion? Explain why you felt the way you did.

3. This chapter presents an assortment of viewpoints on what influences teen sexual behavior. Consider the arguments, then rank them according to which you think are most influential. List any other factors not covered in the chapter that influence teen attitudes about sex.

Chapter 2

1. Frederica Mathewes-Green and the National Campaign to Prevent Teen Pregnancy debate whether teen pregnancy is a serious problem. Which argument do you find more convincing, and why?

2. Authors Michael J. Basso and Judith Levine present arguments on whether sex between underage teens and adults is harmful to teens. Based on your reading of the viewpoint, make a list of the pros and cons of a thirteen-year-old having sex with an adult. What changes would you make to the list if the adolescent was sixteen years old?

Chapter 3

1. This chapter contains two opinions on whether statutory rape laws should be enforced. At what age do you think adolescents should be able to decide for themselves to have sex? Why? Do you think the age should be different for boys and girls? If so, why?

2. There are two opposing viewpoints in this chapter debating whether or not parents should be required to give their consent for an underage teen to have an abortion. If a friend of yours became pregnant, do you think the government should require

one or both of her parents to give their consent to an abortion if your friend wanted one? Explain your answer.

3. Maggie Gallagher and Naomi Seiler debate whether unwed teen mothers should be encouraged to marry. Gallagher argues that marriage would help provide a more stable environment to raise a child. Seiler argues that such marriages would be unstable and would promote conflict in the family. Which position is stronger, in your opinion? Explain.

Chapter 4

1. This chapter contains arguments for and against abstinence-only programs being taught in public schools. Do you think schools should teach teens to abstain from sex until marriage, or do you think that schools should provide more comprehensive sex education programs that include information on birth control? Explain your answer.

2. What type of sex education program does your school have? How effective do you think it is?

3. Linda P. Harvey and Bill Boushka take opposing sides on whether gay, lesbian, bisexual, and transgender issues should be discussed in school sex education programs. Which viewpoint do you agree with, and why?

4. How are gay and lesbian teens treated at your school, both by teachers and other students? What do you think your school could do to provide a safe environment for gay students?

5. In this chapter's final two viewpoints, Heather Boonstra and Meg Meeker debate the role of school sex education classes in teaching students about condom use in preventing the spread of sexually transmitted diseases (STDs). Make a list of the most common STDs and what you think teens should do to insure that they do not become infected.

Organizations to Contact

Advocates for Youth
200 M St. NW, Suite 750, Washington, DC 20036
(202) 419-3420 • fax: (202) 419-1448
e-mail: info@advocatesforyouth.org
Web site: www.advocatesforyouth.org
Advocates for Youth is the only national organization focusing solely on pregnancy and HIV prevention among young people. It provides information, education, and advocacy to youth-serving agencies and professionals, policy makers, and the media. Among the organization's numerous publications are the brochures *Advice from Teens on Buying Condoms* and *Spread the Word—Not the Virus* and the pamphlet *How to Prevent Date Rape: Teen Tips.*

Alan Guttmacher Institute
1301 Connecticut Ave. NW, Suite 700, Washington, DC 20036
(202) 296-4012 • fax: (202) 223-5756
e-mail: info@guttmacher.org • Web site: www.guttmacher.org
The institute works to protect and expand the reproductive choices of all women and men. It strives to ensure that people have access to the information and services they need to exercise their rights and responsibilities concerning sexual activity, reproduction, and family planning. Among the institute's publications are the books *Teenage Pregnancy in Industrialized Countries* and *Today's Adolescents, Tomorrow's Parents: A Portrait of the Americas* and the report "Sex and America's Teenagers."

Coalition for Positive Sexuality (CPS)
3712 N. Broadway, PMB #191, Chicago, IL 60613
(773) 604-1654
Web site: www.positive.org
The Coalition for Positive Sexuality is a grassroots direct-action group formed in the spring of 1992 by high school students and activists. CPS works to counteract what it sees as the institutionalized misogyny, heterosexism, homophobia, racism, and ageism that students experience every day at school. It is dedicated to offering teens sexuality and safe sex education that is pro-woman, pro-lesbian/gay/bisexual, pro–safe sex, and pro-choice. CPS publishes the pamphlet *Just Say Yes* and its Spanish version *¡Di Que Sí!.*

Family Research Council (FRC)
801 G St. NW, Washington, DC 20001
(202) 393-2100 • fax: (202) 393-2134
e-mail: corrdept@frc.org • Web site: www.frc.org

The council is a research, resource, and education organization that promotes the traditional family, which the council defines as a group of people bound by marriage, blood, or adoption. It opposes schools' tolerance of homosexuality and condom distribution programs in schools. It also believes that pornography breaks up marriages and contributes to sexual violence. Among the council's numerous publications are the papers "Revolt of the Virgins," "Abstinence: The New Sexual Revolution," and "Abstinence Programs Show Promise in Reducing Sexual Activity and Pregnancy Among Teens."

Family Resource Coalition of America (FRCA)
205 West Randolph St., Suite 2222, Chicago, IL 60606
(312) 338-0900 • fax: (312) 338-1522
Web site: www.frca.org

FRCA is a national consulting and advocacy organization that seeks to strengthen and empower families and communities so they can foster the optimal development of children, teenagers, and adult family members. FRCA publishes the bimonthly newsletter *Connection*, the report "Family Involvement in Adolescent Pregnancy and Parenting Programs," and the fact sheet "Family Support Programs and Teen Parents."

Focus on the Family
8685 Explorer Dr., Colorado Springs, CO 80920
(719) 531-5181 • fax: (719) 531-3424
Web site: www.family.org

Focus on the Family is an organization that promotes Christian values and strong family ties. It campaigns against pornography and homosexual rights laws. It publishes the monthly magazine *Focus on the Family* and the books *Love Won Out: A Remarkable Journey Out of Homosexuality* and *No Apologies . . . the Truth About Life, Love, and Sex*. It has a Web site for teens, Breakaway, at www.breakawaymag.com.

Gay-Straight Alliance Network
160 Fourteenth St., San Francisco, CA 94103
(415) 552-4229 • fax: (415) 552-4729
e-mail: info@gsanetwork.org • Web site: www.gsanetwork.org

Gay-Straight Alliance Network is a youth-led organization that connects school-based Gay-Straight Alliances (GSAs) to each other and to community resources. Through peer support, leadership development, and training, GSA Network supports young people in starting, strengthening, and sustaining GSAs and builds the capacity of GSAs to create safe environments in schools for students to support each other and learn about homophobia and other oppressions, educate the school community about homophobia, gender identity, and sexual orientation issues, and fight discrimination, harassment, and violence in schools. It publishes the electronic newsletter *GSA Network News.*

Healthy Teen Network
509 Second St. NE, Washington, DC 20002
(202) 547-8814 • fax: (202) 547-8815
e-mail: healthyteens@healthyteennetwork.org
Web site: www.healthyteennetwork.org

Formerly known as the National Organization on Adolescent Pregnancy, Parenting, and Prevention, Healthy Teen Network promotes comprehensive and coordinated services designed for the prevention and resolution of problems associated with adolescent pregnancy and parenthood. It supports families in setting standards that encourage the healthy development of children through loving, stable relationships. Healthy Teen Network publishes various fact sheets on teen pregnancy.

Heritage Foundation
214 Massachusetts Ave. NE, Washington, DC 20002-4999
(202) 546-4400 • fax: (202) 546-8328
e-mail: info@heritage.org • Web site: www.heritage.org

The Heritage Foundation is a public policy research institute that supports the ideas of limited government and the free-market system. It promotes the view that the welfare system has contributed to the problems of illegitimacy and teenage pregnancy. Among the foundation's numerous publications is its Backgrounder series, which includes "Liberal Welfare Programs: What the Data Show on Programs for Teenage Mothers," the paper "Rising Illegitimacy: America's Social Catastrophe," and the bulletin "How Congress Can Protect the Rights of Parents to Raise Their Children."

National Campaign to Prevent Teen Pregnancy
1776 Massachusetts Ave. NW, Suite 200, Washington, DC 20036
(202) 478-8500 • fax: (202) 478-8588
email: campaign@teenpregnancy.org
Web site: www.teenpregnancy.org

The mission of the campaign is to reduce teenage pregnancy by promoting values and activities that are consistent with a pregnancy-free adolescence. The campaign publishes pamphlets, brochures, and opinion polls that include *No Easy Answers: Research Findings on Programs to Reduce Teen Pregnancy, Not Just for Girls: Involving Boys and Men in Teen Pregnancy Prevention, Science Says*, and *Public Opinion Polls and Teen Pregnancy*. Its Web site has an area for teens that includes information that can be downloaded.

Planned Parenthood Federation of America (PPFA)
434 W. Thirty-third St., New York, NY 10001
(212) 541-7800 • (212) 245-1845
e-mail: communications@ppfa.org
Web site: www.plannedparenthood.org

Planned Parenthood believes individuals have the right to control their own fertility without governmental interference. It promotes comprehensive sex education and provides contraceptive counseling and services through clinics across the United States. Its publications include the brochures *Guide to Birth Control: Seven Accepted Methods of Contraception, Teen Sex? It's Okay to Say No Way*, the bimonthly newsletter *LinkLine*, and the online *Choice! Magazine*. It has a Web site for teens at www.teenwire.com.

Project Reality
1701 E. Lake Ave., Suite 371, Glenview, IL 60025
(847) 729-3298 • fax: (847) 729-9744
Web site: www.projectreality.pair.org

Project Reality has developed a sex education curriculum for junior and senior high students called Sex Respect. The program is designed to provide teenagers with information and to encourage sexual abstinence.

Sex, Etc.
Network for Family Life Education, Center for Applied Psychology, Rutgers University
41 Gordon Rd., Suite A, Piscataway, NJ 08854-8067
(732) 445-7929 • fax: (732) 445-7970
email: sexetc@rci.rutgers.edu • Web site: www.sexetc.org

Sex, Etc. is a Web site for teens by teens. It offers information on a wide range of teen sexuality topics, including birth control and condoms, gay and lesbian youth, pregnancy, abortion, and sexually transmitted diseases. It publishes a quarterly electronic newsletter, *Sex, Etc.* Its editorial board is composed entirely of teens.

Sex Information and Education Council of Canada (SIECCAN)

850 Coxwell Ave., Toronto, ON M4C 5R1 Canada

(416) 466-5304 • fax: (416) 778-0785

e-mail: sieccan@web.net • Web site: www.sieccan.org

SIECCAN conducts research on sexual health and sexuality education. It publishes the *Canadian Journal of Human Sexuality*, the resource document *Common Questions About Sexual Health Education*, the booklet *Sexual Health in the Schools: Questions and Answers*, and maintains an information service for health professionals.

Sexuality Information and Education Council of the United States (SIECUS)

130 W. Forty-second St., Suite 350, New York, NY 10036-7802

(212) 819-9770 • fax: (212) 819-9776

e-mail: siecus@siecus.org • Web site: www.siecus.org

SIECUS is an organization of educators, physicians, social workers, and others who support the individual's right to acquire knowledge of sexuality and who encourage responsible sexual behavior. The council promotes comprehensive sex education for all children that includes AIDS education, teaching about homosexuality, and instruction about contraceptives and sexually transmitted diseases. Its publications include fact sheets, annotated bibliographies by topic, the booklet *Talk About Sex*, and the monthly *SIECUS Report*.

Teen-Aid

723 E. Jackson Ave., Spokane, WA 99207

(509) 482-2868 • fax: (509) 482-7994

e-mail: teenaid@teen-aid.org • Web site: www.teen-aid.org

Teen-Aid is an international organization that promotes traditional family values and sexual morality. It publishes a public school sex education curriculum, *Sexuality, Commitment and Family*, stressing sexual abstinence before marriage.

Bibliography of Books

Carolyn E. Cocca — *Jailbait: The Politics of Statutory Rape Laws in the United States.* Albany: State University of New York Press, 2004.

Vicki Courtney — *Teenvirtue: Real Issues, Real Life . . . a Teen Girl's Survival Guide.* Nashville: Broadman & Holman, 2005.

Deborah Davis, ed. — *You Look Too Young to Be a Mom: Teen Mothers Speak Out on Love, Learning, and Success.* New York: Perigee Books, 2004.

Annie Fox and Elizabeth Verdick, ed. — *The Teen Survival Guide to Dating and Relating: Real-World Advice on Guys, Girls, Growing Up, and Getting Along.* Minneapolis: Free Spirit, 2005.

Deborah Hatchell — *What Smart Teenagers Know . . . About Dating, Relationships, and Sex.* Boston: Piper Books, 2003.

Kelly Huegel — *GLBTQ: The Survival Guide for Queer and Questioning Teens.* Minneapolis: Free Spirit, 2003.

Miranda Hunter and William Hunter — *Staying Safe: A Teen's Guide to Sexually Transmitted Diseases.* Brookshire, TX: Mason Crest, 2004.

Janice M. Irvine — *Talk About Sex: The Battles over Sex Education in the United States.* Berkeley: University of California Press, 2004.

Roger J.R. Levesque, ed. — *Sexuality Education: What Adolescents' Rights Require.* Hauppauge, NY: Nova Science, 2003.

Judith Levine — *Harmful to Minors: The Perils of Protecting Children from Sex.* New York: Thunder's Mouth Press, 2003.

David Levithan — *Boy Meets Boy.* New York: Knopf, 2003.

Hal Marcovitz — *Teens and Sex.* Brookshire, TX: Mason Crest, 2004.

Meg Meeker — *Epidemic: How Teen Sex Is Killing Our Kids.* Washington, DC: Lifeline Press, 2002.

Sylvia Olsen — *The Girl with a Baby.* Winlaw, British Columbia, Canada: Sono NIS Press, 2004.

Jim Pollard and Chloe Kent — *Sex.* Chicago: Raintree, 2005.

Lynn Ponton — *The Sex Lives of Teenagers: Revealing the Secret World of Adolescent Boys and Girls.* New York: Plume, 2001.

Mary Louise Rasmussen, Eric Rofes, and Susan Talburt, eds.	*Youth and Sexualities: Pleasure, Subversion, and Insubordination in and out of Schools.* New York: Palgrave Macmillan, 2004.
Jason Rich	*Growing Up Gay in America.* Portland, OR: Franklin Street Books, 2002.
Patricia Roles	*Facing Teen Pregnancy: A Handbook for the Pregnant Teen.* Washington, DC: Child Welfare League of America Press, 2004.
Ritch C. Savin-Williams	*The New Gay Teenager.* Cambridge, MA: Harvard University Press, 2005.
Deborah A. Stanley	*Sexual Health Information for Teens: Health Tips About Sexual Development, Human Reproduction, and Sexually Transmitted Diseases.* Detroit: Omnigraphics, 2003.
Pam Stenzel	*Sex Has a Price Tag.* Grand Rapids, MI: Zondervan, 2003.
Deborah L. Tolman	*Dilemmas of Desire: Teenage Girls Talk About Sexuality.* Cambridge, MA: Harvard University Press, 2005.
Sabrina Weill	*The Real Truth About Teens and Sex: From Hooking Up to Friends with Benefits—What Teens Are Thinking, Doing, and Talking About, and How to Help Them Make Smart Choices.* New York: Perigee Trade, 2005.
William L. Yarber	*STDs and HIV: A Guide for Today's Teens.* Reston, VA: American Alliance for Health, Physical Education, Recreation, and Dance, 2003.
Franklin E. Zimring	*An American Travesty: Legal Responses to Adolescent Sexual Offending.* Chicago: University of Chicago Press, 2004.

Index